A Letter to Forerunners

Experiencing a Revelatory Reformation

Book II
Kings and Queens of Creation

Luc Niebergall

Printed in the United States of America

First Edition, 2013

ISBN-10: 1492358401
ISBN-13: 978-1492358404

Kingdom Revelation Publishing

Dedication

I dedicate this book to every believer in the body of Christ. We are in a great time of advancement and expansion of God's kingdom. You are not called on the sidelines of what God is doing on the earth today. You are pivotal to His plan and irreplaceable in His heart.

Table Of Contents

Introduction

I wrote this book for many reasons. From one perspective I wrote this for those of you who have a burden to see heaven invade earth. My heart is to help unveil your importance by presenting how powerful you truly are. I believe God wants to expand your understanding of how much influence you carry by maximizing confidence in your heavenly identity.

From another perspective, I wrote for those of you who have experienced an internal revival, yet don't live in a culture where your passion and fire are accepted or celebrated. I wrote for those in the prophetic community who have in any way felt on the side lines of the church because of their callings or giftings. This is a letter to anyone who feels alone and separate from the family of God.

A Letter To Forerunners

My declaration throughout this teaching is that forerunners, prophetic people and the isolated will be reconciled and grafted back into the family of God. I would ask that you take my hand and walk with me into a greater revelation of how accepted and celebrated you truly are in God's kingdom. You are not alone.

Lastly, I wrote to bring clarity concerning the true foundation of Christ. I believe we are on the brink of a new season, where God will be releasing profound and pivotal truths to the body of Christ which will transcend our former understanding. My heart is to unveil to you your revelatory access throughout this book. In order to steward revelation properly, it is important that we first comprehend our foundation before we begin building upon it. For those of us who have begun experiencing an internal revival, we carry the responsibility of allowing the full foundation to be established within us. We carry responsibility because we have become forerunners of the revival which has been birthed within us. We carry responsibility because if we try to lead from an understanding of the foundation in part instead of whole, it can potentially bring more destruction than edification. As our revelation concerning the complete foundation enhances we will have the wisdom to lead from a place of integrity and love.

I pray that Spirit of Wisdom and Revelation will rest upon each person who reads this book. Holy Spirit, lead each person into a deep relationship with You. Lead them into the fullness of Christ and into the loving arms of the Father.

The Honoured Forerunner

Creation embraced me as I hiked its stony paths throughout the Kananaskis Mountains of Alberta. The sun shone on me like a smile, offering hospitality as I ventured throughout nature's well-kept home. Each step I took was followed by the shelter of greater peace. Solitude granted me with a gift of stillness, allowing the depths of my heart to harmonize with my Creator's. He talked sweetly, permitting His deep affection and love towards me to spill forth from His mouth. He clothed me with acceptance and unveiled confidence from within that confirmed my sonship. With words that sailed upon His voice, He peeled a layer off of the word 'intimacy' exposing its eternal depth. Like the loving Father He is, He led me through His vast mountains with excellence, knowing every nook and detail.

As He led me throughout the elaborate trails, my attention wandered to the right, targeting a small part of a mountain. The small mountain stood proud at about 40 feet. Since it looked climbable, I left the comfort of the path, and accepting creation's challenge started my ascent. Peace intoxicated me as I climbed the colossal rock.

Halfway up my climb, I was unexpectedly interrupted by the voice of a man from behind. He broke the silence by asking me a question. He asked, *"When Moses climbed Mount Sinai, do you think it was an easy, paved climb or a strenuous one?"* I stuck close and still, glued to the face of the rock knowing that previous to that moment there was no one around for at least a few miles. I turned around to see the face of the man who spoke to me. Standing back on the trail was a man whose presence projected significant importance. The hair that fell to the sides of his face was matted and pressed tightly to his cheeks, while the hair on the top of his head, filled with so much dirt and sweat, stood unnaturally high. He wore a ratty garment made of camel's hair which was worn in contrast to his radiant smile. I knew instantly that standing before me was John the Baptist.

Making my way down the outcropping of rock, I headed back to the path towards John. I was thanking God over and over again for the honour I would have to meet one of the greatest forerunners who had ever walked the earth.

As distance decreased between John and I, he met me with an inviting smile that widened, trumping his former one. John asked me again, *"When Moses climbed Mount Sinai do you think it was an easy, paved climb or a strenuous one?"* His voice was as hard as stone, refined by persistent certainty. Yet when he spoke, compassion and love were unmistakably seen in his eyes.

"I would assume that it would have been strenuous," I replied.

"Ah, so can be the road that a forerunner travels," John said. *"When you are a forerunner, you walk a road that has never been paved by anyone. You are the pioneer. Though when you perceive the weight of the truth which will be discovered, you understand that perseverance is a small price to pay. As a forerunner you must always remember who you are walking with. When you know that Jesus walks with you and carries the burden, the road becomes easy and light."*

John's voice trailed off for a few moments, permitting time to carry his words deeper into my heart. He allowed the silence to linger, and then continued on with his teaching:

"The Israelites would look up at Mount Sinai to witness the thundering, the flashes of lightening, the sound of the trumpet and the smoke of the Lord. When they saw God's power and glory they would stand far off in fear. Where the Israelites saw the mountain that was covered in thick darkness as something to be avoided, Moses saw it as something to be pursued. He was able to do this because he was looking through the lens of someone who was hungry for the mysteries of God. Instead of seeing the thick darkness as something that was unapproachable, Moses saw it as the deep and undiscovered things of God" (Exodus 20:18-21).

"This will be the heart posture of anyone who will be used to forerun a revelation. Out of a hunger to know the deep things of God, they will be willing to embrace truth which may at first be feared by others. They will

15

look at the unclimbable mountain and allow their passionate hunger to defy impossibility. Some will at times fear pursuing truth because it may cost what is familiar to them. But, we need to heed wisdom by learning to step beyond what is comfortable to us. A past revelation can cradle us for a time, but as we grow older we need to step beyond our cribs to expand our knowledge of life. God is eternal, and His revelation is endless."

John continued, *"On one occasion Moses brought the seventy elders of Israel up with him onto Mount Sinai. Together they encountered the God of Israel in His heavenly splendour"* (Exodus 24:9-18). *"Moses was then called by God to higher places on the mountain, where he received the revelation of the law. Since he was the first to receive the revelation, this made him the law's forerunner. He received the Ten Commandments written on stone slabs, which were taken from a part of the mountain that only Moses had climbed."*

"Moses did the work of climbing the mountain to receive fragments of stone from the top, while the Israelites stayed behind out of fear. Although Moses did all of the work, his desire to obey God permitted the Israelites to also receive the stone from the heights of the mountain. Even though a forerunner does the work of paving the road, generations get to walk through with ease to experience the fruit of his or her obedience. Every humble leader will allow the studious to stand on their shoulders to partake in the same blessings that they themselves do."

John and I then walked in the quiet of summer for a time without saying a word. As a refined teacher, it seemed as though he used silence as a tool, giving me the opportunity to meditate on each lesson he taught.

John would look at the different aspects of nature and laugh occasionally, as though God were telling him jokes through His creation. His clear appreciation for nature demonstrated someone who was in a direct relationship with God the Creator.

"All of creation prophesies and glorifies Jesus" John said. *"As lovers of Christ, our eyes need to be in a constant pursuit to see Him continually. Every forerunner needs to live in this place of constant communion with God the Creator."*

As soon as the words left his mouth, a cool wind swept into the air changing the personality of the weather. The temperature went from being a sunny summer day to a blizzard within less than 10 seconds. Suddenly my choice of wearing shorts for a hike in +30 degrees blew up in my face as I stood shivering in -25 degrees.

"Every forerunner needs to learn to live in two places at once" John said. *"The cold temperature is symbolic of how an unreceptive culture will treat a forerunner. If those who are forerunners can only see the winter then they will feel its effects. Even though their bodies may live in the cold of winter, in their spirits and souls they need to constantly be experiencing the warmth of intimacy with God the Creator. They need to feast off of the revelation of His beauty. Once the warmth of intimacy is solidified within their hearts, in due time they will be given influence and platform to*

release what they know in their spirit man into the natural. The warmth will then prevail over the cold, shifting the atmosphere and transforming a culture."

John then spoke aloud again saying the word, *"summer"*. Instantly a warm wind blew in through the trees, which quickly restored the weather back to its original snowless state.

I stood dumbfounded looking at John, shocked at the honour of getting to sit under the teaching of someone who Jesus held in such high regard. John looked back at me, gave me a wide smile and then disappeared.

Set Apart As Sign Posts

A profound truth which is being solidified within the heart of Jesus' bride is the revelation of the forerunners of Christ. The encounter I had when I met John the Baptist which you just read, is a prophetic declaration of the forerunner anointing which is being deposited into the church. A forerunner is a person who will walk in a revelation which others haven't yet received. They see another side of the face of Jesus and will more than likely be called to help prepare the body of Christ to receive that same revelation. Forerunners have seen ahead of time what God has ordained the entire church to walk in for the future and are living out that revelation in their present lives. They have seen the bride's potential and walk in that potential in the now. They stand as spiritual signposts to show the rest of the body that there is still a higher standard of life that they can live. Through their obedience in living out the understanding they have received, they plow the way for generations to come through the doors they have opened.

A Letter To Forerunners

Some of you who have received a revelation of revival may notice that others around you aren't walking in the same understanding. You may notice that others are perceiving life through a different lens than yourself. This is because God has given you a new set of eyes to see. You are perceiving life's circumstances through eyes which expect heaven to invade earth. You are seeing people with love and compassion because your heart is harmonizing with your Father's. You are purposefully set apart. What a wonderful honour. Whether you are experiencing this in your job, your family, or even the church, all that this means is you are one of the first fruits of revival in your present surroundings. You have been commissioned as a forerunner of truth to run forth with the word that God has rooted in your heart.

I have a big heart for this generation of forerunners. Just as all of you who are reading this book, I have walked as one myself ever since I was birthed into salvation. I have seen what many of the pitfalls look like and have learned to overcome them with the council of Holy Spirit. The call of a forerunner isn't limited to those who will forerun a fresh revelation to the global church. We are living in a time where God is unveiling a vast number of forerunners that He is releasing to restore truth. Where before, it seemed to be the few who were standing in the gap for generations, now that the unveiling of forerunners is taking place, we are discovering that the mantle of a forerunner isn't just for the select, but for the entire body of Christ. Where some stand as signposts which will mark restored revelations for the church with global influence, others will be forerunners before their families with a revelation of Christ to lead them into the Father's arms. Some will express fresh revelation of God's love to the point where entire cities will be transformed into the kingdom of heaven. Every one of us is called to be a forerunner of the love of Jesus where awareness of His love is scarce.

The vastness of the forerunner calling is a wonderful thing. While we are all called to forerun revival and fresh revelation, every single one of us in the body of Christ is also a forerunner of the image of God. What I mean by this is, the world tries to classify and categorize each person, but the truth is that we are all uniquely wonderful. We are all forerunners in one way or another because we all reflect a unique side of the personality of God. No one has ever lived a life like you live with Jesus. This means that every one of us in at least one aspect, is most likely misunderstood and stands apart different from our fellow man. We all directly reflect the image of God who is often misunderstood, therefore are forerunners of a unique perspective of who God is.

As we journey together, with the help of Holy Spirit, my heart is to lay out a teaching that will help you to function as a forerunner from a place of victory and honour.

Just as John the Baptist foreran the first coming of the Messiah, as the body of Christ we get to forerun the second coming. We are the Elijah generation. We get to plow the way for Christ's coming by reflecting the image of God through the diversity of the church's personality and revelation.

Partnering With Spirit Of Revelation

In many ways fresh revelation will mark a forerunner. It's a forerunner's fresh perspective of who God is that sets him or her apart. John the Baptist was the greatest forerunner who ever lived under the Old Covenant because he foreran the coming of the Messiah.

Before John was embraced by Israel as a prophet to teach the message of repentance, he was first commissioned into the desert where he received the revelation. Revelation is experiential knowledge. You can hear the truth that Jesus loves you over and over again, understanding it intellectually in your mind, but revelation is when truth moves from being knowledge to an encounter in your heart. When we truly receive a

23

revelation it becomes part of us permitting us to view life through that particular lens of truth. Right when we start our relationship with Holy Spirit, we begin to partner with Him by receiving revelation. We begin to be taught by Spirit of Revelation as He leads us into the deep things of God.

Spirit of Revelation is one of the seven Spirits of God before God's throne (Revelation 1:4). Other than in the book of Revelation, the seven Spirits are mentioned in the book of Isaiah.

Isaiah 11:2: *"The Spirit of the LORD shall rest upon Him, the Spirit of wisdom and understanding (revelation), the Spirit of counsel and might, the Spirit of knowledge and of the fear of the LORD."*

The seven Spirits of God aren't actually seven separate spirits. Notice how 'S' in 'Spirit' is capital and not lowercase, showing that it is speaking of God instead of celestial beings. Seven in prophetic numerology is the number of completion since the world was completed in seven days. This shows us that the seven Spirits of God is referring to the manifold ministry of Holy Spirit.

Spirit of Revelation abides in us (Romans 8:11). Scripture also says that the seven Spirits of God are before the throne of God (Revelation 1:4). This is the same throne which we can boldly approach at anytime we please (Hebrews 4:16), showing that our revelatory maturity is dependent on how close we are willing to come to the Lamb. Spirit of Revelation didn't come to descend and ascend. He came to rest and make us His dwelling place, giving us an eternal access to understanding.

In Revelation 4, the four living creatures would worship God day and night. I find it interesting that this chapter says God made the four living creatures covered with eyes. He gave them the privilege to constantly gaze upon the Lamb of God. They are always observing His nature, growing in understanding of who He is. The four living creatures, although covered with eyes never grow tired in worshipping God because He never ceases to give fresh revelation. The twenty four elders can forever bow down saying, *"You are worthy, Oh Lord!"* because every time they look up, they see a fresh perspective of who God is. The eternal God never ceases to give fresh revelation because He is endless.

When Adam ate fruit from the tree of the knowledge of good and evil, he received a revelation of what good and evil were. It only makes sense that if he received revelation of what good and evil were when he ate from the tree of the knowledge of good and evil, that when he ate fruit from the tree of life he would have received a revelation of life. This means that as hungry as Adam became, he could eat and grow in understanding. As hungry as you allow yourself to become, you can taste the goodness of God and grow in your revelatory maturity.

Ephesians 1:15-18: *"Therefore I also, after I heard of your faith in the Lord Jesus and your love for all the saints, do not cease to give thanks for you, making mention of you in my prayers: that the God of our Lord Jesus Christ, the Father of glory, may give to you the spirit of wisdom and revelation in the knowledge of Him, the eyes of your understanding being enlightened; that you may know what is the hope of His calling, what are the riches of the glory of His inheritance in the saints".*

As we receive fresh revelation the eyes of our understanding opens (Ephesians 1:18), just as when Adam and Eve ate from the tree of the knowledge of good and evil. Genesis 3:7 says, *"The eyes of both of them were opened."* When Adam and Eve obtained revelation after eating the fruit, they forever perceived the world through their new set of eyes. Their understanding of life and circumstance was interpreted differently because they looked through an entirely new lens. We always see life through whichever lens of revelation we carry. This is why forerunners are set apart by the revelation they have allowed to sink into their understanding.

Creativity Births Fresh Revelation

Adam had a profound revelation of God the Creator since he saw creation unfolding first hand. Since he was able to receive the aspect of God who creates, Adam could also see creativity within himself. When we see God and understand Him, we see and understand ourselves because we are created in His image. Adam was so creative he could actually name every species of animal without using the same name twice (Genesis 2:20).

As we pursue fresh revelation, it's important that we understand God in the aspect of Creator. When we honour God as Creator, we are receiving Him as one who brings beginning and newness. The reason why this is important is because we become what we encounter. When we worship God as the Creator, a spirit of creativity is released. When creativity is released, we become open to new ideas and fresh truths.

I always hear people say, *"We shouldn't put God in a box"*. When in actuality, God hasn't been in a box since the Old Testament when He dwelled in the Ark of the Covenant. God is too big to box up. We are the ones who have been barricaded and caged from truth by complacency and an unhealthy soul-tie to familiarity. We need to heed wisdom by learning to step beyond what is comfortable to us. A past revelation can cradle us for a time, but as we grow older we need to step beyond our cribs to expand our knowledge of life. God is eternal, and His revelation is endless. When we make the decision to excel in our creativity, we are prone to venturing where others haven't yet travelled. God's heart is a vast place waiting to be discovered.

This is often where many get stuck concerning their revelatory maturity. We grow accustomed to past truths, therefore fear pursuing new ones. This is actually how new denominations start. Every denomination was birthed when God first restored a new truth back to the church. Now, when God reveals the next new truth to the church there are some who will embrace it and some who will reject it. For those who embrace it, they move forward growing in understanding and moving on where the Lord is moving. Those who reject it stay behind still feeding off of past revelation that was once new to them. This is when a singular group separates into two creating several different theologies. This is why there are so many churches with so many different doctrines. Division in the church in many ways is the by-product of not receiving Spirit of Revelation's ministry in our lives. We can't go on trying to live off of yesterday's manna. There is a release of new bread from heaven every day. We need to constantly be moving forward with Holy Spirit in the revelation He is revealing.

Have you ever wondered why John was called John the Baptist? It's interesting because even though John was a prophet, he isn't known as 'the prophet John' as his forefather prophets from the Old Testament are known. It's the same with the apostle John. Even though the other apostles were best known as apostles, John is better known as John the Revelator or John the Beloved. The reason why both John the Baptist and John the Revelator differed in ministerial titles compared to their peers in office, is because there was something in their ministries which was so unique it completely changed how history remembers them. John the Baptist was used as a prophet, but the gem of his ministry was the revelation of the baptism of repentance. This creative revelation separated him from his forefather prophets. John the Revelator was a profoundly great apostle and prophet, but he is better known as 'the Beloved' who was entrusted with the secrets of Christ's return because of the revelation he carried to receive a unique message.

Ezekiel 2:9-10, 3:1-3: *"Now when I looked, there was a hand stretched out to me; and behold, a scroll of a book was in it. Then He spread it before me; and there was writing on the inside and on the outside, and written on it were lamentations of mourning and woe. Moreover He said to me, 'son of man eat, eat what you find; eat this scroll, and go, speak to the house of Israel.' So I opened my mouth, and He caused me to eat that scroll. And He said to me, 'son of man, feed your belly, and fill your stomach with this scroll that I give you.' So I ate, and it was in my mouth like honey in sweetness."*

God is handing out honey scrolls to His church. The entire prophetic message recorded throughout the book of Ezekiel is the unfolding of what was written on the scroll Ezekiel ate. God is looking for a people who will consume the word, and then speak it out just as Ezekiel did. There is an increase of culture changing revelation coming. The reasoning behind this is because there has been a swift acceleration of forerunners who are committed to walking in their revelatory access. There has been an increase of saints who have made the decision to venture into the undiscovered realms of the heart of God. Not only will these forerunners walk in revelatory access, but I believe also an increase of acceptance from the body of Christ. There will be acceleration in a forerunner's acceptance because I believe the church is coming to a place of maturity where we are learning to receive Jesus however He chooses to come. It's interesting to note that Ezekiel was given a scroll from a book, implying that Ezekiel only received a small fragment of an entire book of revelation. We see and know in part, therefore we need the revelation God reveals through the whole church.

Since the body of Christ is tremendously diverse in revelation and personality, some forerunners may be labelled as being dramatic and eccentric; but so were many great men and women of God who were written about throughout biblical history. People could have used the fact that John the Baptist wore camel's hair, ate locusts and shouted messages from the desert as means to dismiss the message. But, those who were hungry enough for God's truth received the messenger out of a desire to receive God's Word. When God is doing a new thing it may at times seem flamboyant, but we shouldn't dismiss the Word of the Lord because of eccentric personalities.

We are living in a time where God is going to begin to raise up men and women of God, where heaven's expression through them will be so original that it will paint the nations with colours the world has never before seen. As the church embraces the vast messages, they will be displayed as unique gem stones to beautify Jesus' bride for her wedding day.

We can see all throughout church history that God raising up forerunners is a pattern He uses to firmly establish a truth within the church. Back before the 1500's, our accessibility to receive grace was a foreign concept to the body of Christ. So, God rose up Martin Luther as a great forerunner to restore the lost truth. Now in the present day, grace is becoming common logic to believers and the teaching is vastly received. This is outstanding considering that back when Martin Luther would teach about grace, riots would break out because it was so controversial. In order for this breakthrough to take place, a forerunner had to allow truth to become so real to him that he couldn't help but stand boldly amongst an unreceptive culture. Unflinchingly he looked persecution in the eyes and proudly proclaimed a revelation that would alter history forever.

God rose up Charles Parham in the early 1900's to restore the revelation that there is still power in speaking in tongues. While at the time he was labelled as a heretic because of his teachings, now this theology is beginning to be widely received. Forerunners like Smith Wigglesworth, Maria Woodworth-Etter, Evan Roberts and Kathryn Kuhlman were used in the 'Voice of Healing Movement' to demonstrate that Jesus still wants to use the church as a vessel for healing. Every time God wants to restore a revelation to the church he will raise up a person or ministry to forerun the truth by teaching it and walking it out.

Michelangelo Buonarroti is a forerunner who I immensely respect and admire. Although he didn't forerun a revelation within the church, through the arts he released divine inspiration to transform culture in the late 1400's and early 1500's. When Michelangelo sculpted the statue of David, he had it in his heart to present an image that portrayed mankind as still being beautiful because he was created in the image of God. He sculpted David as a statement that mankind had worth and value. It has been documented on numerous occasions, of people falling on their knees weeping before the statue because a revelation of self-worth hit them as they looked upon David.

As you partner with Holy Spirit by receiving revelation, be willing to step out of any familiarity you may have entrenched yourself in. Look forth beyond worldly logic into the unknown and engulf yourself in adventure. God's destiny over you is that you will know the deep things of His heart. His will is that you would comprehend His friendship, so He can share His profound secrets with you. Receive a revelation of God the Creator, because in that you dethrone monotony and live a life of constant newness as you forever discover the diversity of God's eternal nature.

Marrying Wisdom To Revelation

Nurturing Revelation

Many people will start their initial revelatory journey by receiving what other ministries carry. I've met many people who would go off on mission trips, or to different churches to experience the love of God through the expression of revival. Their eyes would be opened to seeing heaven invade earth in a way that set them completely on fire. When they would come back home, they notice that their revelatory knowledge doesn't fit into their old system of living life. This is because they have grown up into a greater place of spiritual maturity. Whereas their past surroundings at one point felt comfortable, after experiencing God in a greater glory, their former environment now felt as though it threatened to cage their passion.

I have also met many forerunners who received their understanding in the secret place with God, instead of receiving revelation from another ministry. Their hunger wouldn't allow them to have anything less than the depths of God's heart. This of course separated them from the world's way of life and pushed them to live like the citizens of heaven they were created to be. They became set apart because they viewed life with a completely different set of eyes.

Sometimes what will happen is a new revelation will birth within us, but the culture which is familiar to us won't receive it. Every one of us is called to influence and change cultures through the revelation we carry. However, one of the pitfalls a forerunner needs to watch out for is allowing their surrounding culture to influence them by killing the revelatory seed.

I've met many people who when they walked with specific ministries or mission organizations would easily be able to keep the fire of revival burning. They would move powerfully in miracles, signs and wonders. However, when they would come out from that environment their fire would burn out and they would stop pressing for the miraculous. Have you ever been around a profound man or woman of God and felt a newness where you could actually feel your faith level increase while being around them? Have you felt that after a few days of not being in their presence or under their teaching your faith goes back to its former state? I'm pretty sure all of us have experienced this to some extent. I'm going to tell you why this happens and how you can avoid this pitfall.

One of my primary anointings is to train and equip the church to hear the voice of God and to move in miracles, signs and wonders. When people come to courses I teach, even if they have never heard God speak to them, they will begin to hear the voice of God. They will start having visions, dreams, and prophetic encounters. Even if they have never prayed for anyone to be healed, when I teach and activate them they see Jesus healing through their own hands.

I can't count how many people have come to me a week after one of my courses had finished to tell me that ever since the class stopped, they haven't been able to prophesy as accurately or as consistently as they did in class. Or they would say they haven't had the same fire to press in to see the miraculous. This is why:

The reason why people can instantly walk in these things of the Spirit when they come under my covering is because I have made all of these manifestations of the kingdom a part of my daily life. I see miracles on a regular basis. Hearing the voice of God is one of the most important things to my heart. I've cultivated a lifestyle of visions, dreams and prophetic encounters. People who come under my covering are actually stepping into a culture I have created internally for myself. It's nearly impossible to not experience a well established culture if you are standing right in the middle of it. This is why when people are around me they will experience in that moment what is my daily reality. My culture invades their normal. They are having a taste of my daily bread.

When people step out of this type of covering it feels harder to tap into the same things because they are stepping out of a culture where it is common. Here's what we need to understand; even when we step out of an established culture, there has still been seeds of revelation deposited within our spirits. When we make the decision to stop watering the seed, the seed of revelation which was birthed within us doesn't grow because we didn't know how to mother the seed properly; therefore it dies. We actually need to learn to allow the seed to develop into an internal culture. Once this happens, our internal culture will shift the external making it bow to the will and order of God.

It's good to be teachable to receive what others carry, but our revelatory standpoint can't be dependent on being around others because we are all in direct relationship with Spirit of Revelation. Many of us in the church have been submitting to an unhealthy co-dependence. It's fine if a new-born Christian needs to be sustained by Sunday morning services; but it's not okay if we have been saved for 10 years to be dependent on our leaders or meetings to sustain our personal relationship with Jesus or the revelation we carry. We can't allow ourselves to become so co-dependent on other ministries or ministers to the point where we can't steward what was given to us apart from them. God is looking for people who will honour the truth that Holy Spirit has given them. We honour truth by watering it and by wielding it to produce fruit. As your internal revelation solidifies, people around you will begin to experience what you carry, and their experience will be the fruit of your stewardship.

Patience And Pearls

I'm a firm believer that when we first receive a revelation from God the best way to steward it is to share it with someone else. Although there is truth to this, we need to allow wisdom to wield our zeal in who we share with and the timing of it, otherwise unnecessary damage can be done. There is great restlessness which can grip a forerunner. One of the mindsets a forerunner needs to avoid is trying to step onto his or her platform before God has ordained it. Zeal without wisdom can often push a forerunner into stressing to find immediate platform to speak the message. How busy we are is a terrible way to grid our success, considering that Jesus was never in a panic to change the world. He trusted His Father's agenda and timing. Jesus waited 30 years to be released into His ministry on earth.

A tip of wisdom which needs to be rooted in a forerunner's way of thinking is to not cast your pearls before swine (Matthew 7:6). There are two key reasons to heed this wisdom. The first is that when we scatter God's word in a place where it won't be received, it will likely be trampled on. Joseph was a prime example of someone who surrendered his pearls due to unharnessed zeal when he shared his prophetic dream to his brothers without God's instruction. Even though the word he presented to them was truth, Joseph's brothers' hearts weren't yet fertile enough to receive the word. Not being wise in sharing God's word cost Joseph years of trouble (Genesis 37).

Moses had the same problem as a forerunner. When he was walking in the desert he saw an Egyptian fighting an Israelite. Out of a love and desire to see Israel walking in freedom from their current slavery, he struck the Egyptian dead (Exodus 2:11-12). Later on, this act of passion got Moses in trouble with his own people. See, God had already placed in Moses' heart the burden that He wanted to deliver the Israelites, but Moses tried to start the revolution of Exodus before its ordained time. We can clearly see the contrast of success 40 years later when Moses, as an activist contended for Israel's freedom in the proper timing. If we aren't able to guard God's word properly, not only does the message face unnecessary persecution, so does the messenger.

The second reason why we shouldn't cast pearls before swine is that pearls are round, so therefore the swine will slip on them. We don't want something that's a blessing to us to become a stumbling block to someone else just because we don't know how to steward what was given to us with integrity. Mark 1:42-45 gives clear indication of this:

"As soon as He (Jesus) had spoken, immediately the leprosy left him, and he was cleansed. And He strictly warned him and sent him away at once, and said to him, 'See that you say nothing to anyone, but go your way, show yourself to the priest, and offer for your cleansing those things which Moses commanded, as a testimony to them.' However, he went out and began to proclaim it freely, and to spread the matter, so that Jesus could no longer openly enter the city, but was outside in deserted places; and they came to Him from every direction."

When Jesus cleansed the man of leprosy, the former leper was commissioned as a forerunner of the knowledge of Christ. Jesus, knowing that the people's hearts in the city weren't yet ripe enough to receive Him, commanded the man to remain silent. Jesus understood that it can be necessary for a forerunner to be hidden for a season to allow the culture around them to be readied to be recipients of the word. Instead of listening to Jesus, the forerunner's excitement drove him to speak freely of what had happened to him. Although the man's intent was to spread awareness of Christ, the foreknowledge of the miracle closed a door for Jesus to have any platform in the city. Instead He was banned outside in deserted places, lessening His potential to eventually minister to a greater mass of people because the former leper didn't wield his revelation with wisdom.

Sometimes when I'm invited as a guest to speak at a church, God will specifically tell me to not share specific revelation. It's not because He doesn't want that particular church to walk in the same revelation. It's usually because they aren't yet ready to receive that specific truth in their hearts. There is a time to release revelation, however a forerunner needs to come under the council of Holy Spirit to know when the appropriate time is to share God's message.

Many years ago on one of my trips to heaven, I was guided by the same two angels who had previously toured me through heaven, time and time again. The angel on my right was named Daniel, where the angel on my left as far as I knew was nameless. Whenever I would try to look at the angel's face on my left, the celestial being's face would instantly distort not permitting me to distinguish an identity. I saw great signs and wonders throughout the heavens on my tour. After a few hours of heavenly sight-seeing, Daniel asked me where I would like to go. I responded instantly putting in a request to see the heavenly courts (Daniel 7:9-10, Job 1:6-12, 1 Kings 22:19-22). Daniel began to tell me that it is usually only those who are summoned who are brought to the heavenly courts, but since I was one of the sons of God, he would lead me there.

When we arrived at the courts of heaven, I stood before the building's intimidating doors which stood over 100 feet tall. I pulled on one of the hard doorhandles surprised at how I could move such a colossal door. I strode into the court room to see thousands of angels seated on ornamented seats shaped in a semicircle. Seated in the centre of the room was my King, Jesus.

Some of the greater angels were talking amongst one another discussing revival strategy for specific states within the United States of America. As they talked, Jesus looked over at me and smiled:

"What is on your heart, Luc?" Jesus asked.

At this point in my life, I had walked as a forerunner of revival for a few years, and like many forerunners, a great restlessness was being stirred within me to release the message God had given me.

I told Jesus, *"Lord, It's burning in my heart to be in ministry to train and equip Your church."*

Jesus laughed and said, *"It's not your time yet for ministry. I'm in the process of preparing you to speak, and I'm preparing my bride to receive the message I have placed within you."*

Jesus then noted to the angel called Daniel to lead me out of the heavenly courts. The angel grabbed me and began to usher me out of the building.

For the next few days after this encounter my restlessness to bring change still agitated me. In my zeal, I would engage heaven and would consistently ask the angels to lead me back to the heavenly courts. I would ask Jesus the same question as I previously asked just to receive the exact same answer over and over again.

On my sixth and final time approaching God concerning what I was currently wrestling within my heart, I stood again in the great courts of heaven.

Jesus again looked over at me and asked the same question which always followed my visit, *"What is on your heart, Luc?"*

I looked at Jesus and said to Him, *"I know that it's not my time to share Your message yet to the church. Bring me into a season where I can be trained to lead from a place of wisdom and integrity."*

Jesus gave me another loving smile and said, *"Luc, I am so proud of you. You will release the message in due time. Until then I will walk with you as I always have to train you in the ways of the Father's heart."*

Instead of waiting for Jesus to motion for Daniel to usher me out, I walked out willingly. I pushed open the huge doors and departed. When I was outside, I was surprised to see that the angel called Daniel wasn't with me anymore. He was nowhere to be seen. Standing before me was the angel who always stood on my left whose face I could never see. I looked intently at His face until clarity befriended my sight. I was greatly moved when I saw that what I thought was an angel guiding for years throughout heaven, was in fact Jesus.

Jesus spoke to me and said, *"Walk with Me and I will continue to train you in the ways of the Father's heart."*

Forerunners have seasons of exposure as well as hiddenness. If we don't discern and honour the seasons which God has called us, we could end up doing the right thing in the wrong time. Honour your times of hiddenness. Many leaders burn out and experience fall-outs from ministry because they force their way onto a platform their character can't yet steward. Meekness means walking in a humble patience, just as Jesus did only as He saw His Father do (John 5:19-20). Those who carry this attribute are the ones who God entrusts with the nations (Matthew 5:5).

David was appointed to be king in 1 Samuel 16. When David was mantled as king of Israel, he didn't begin reigning as a king in Israel until 11 years later. This is remarkable because it shows us that even though in the eyes of man David wasn't in a position of kingship, God viewed David as a king even though he was still a shepherd. As you progress through your seasons of training, it is important to know that God doesn't view you through the lens of what you've done. He sees you for who you were created to be even if you aren't yet walking on your highest place of platform. Your calling is in the hand of God, not of man. Take the time to remind yourself of who He has created you to be. Hold close the message He has placed within your heart. Meditate on the prophetic words that have been spoken over you. As a forerunner, John the Baptist didn't remain in his season of receiving revelation. There was an ordained time where he was embraced by Israel to speak the revelation God entrusted to him.

Four Corners Of The True Foundation

In a dream I had a few years ago, I saw a congregation of 200 people in the foyer of a church fellowshipping. The pastor of the church heard a loud noise coming from outside and immediately went to see what the source of the noise was. The pastor with his congregation huddled in front of the glass doors. As they looked, a tornado approached the church and stood in front of the entrance of the building. The tornado took complete attention from every eye. As the pastor and congregation watched attentively, they began to notice that the tornado didn't cause any damage to the building itself, but instead was chipping away at the concrete foundation the church was built upon.

When forerunners are living out the revelation they have received, in a revelatory state they can in many ways stand separate from the church. If the church isn't in a state of receptiveness towards the message, then instead of the forerunners getting to directly deposit the revelation they carry, they will instead teach the church to observe through their actions. As the church observes, the forerunners through living out the message begin to prepare the body to receive new aspects of God. As forerunners live lives which reflect the revelation they carry, they tear up any false foundations that have been built within the observers hearts which stand in contrast to the true foundation, which is Christ.

This was actually one of John the Baptist's roles as a forerunner to Christ's coming. Luke 3:5 says that John's ministry was to see that *"every valley shall be filled and every mountain and hill brought low; the crooked places shall be made straight and the rough ways smooth."* John went forth with a message of repentance. When the Israelites would gather and take part in John's baptism there was a mass restoration of Israel coming into a form of right standing with God. When this move of repentance took place, healing began to sweep throughout the history of the land. Every valley was filled and every mountain and hill was bought low. The crooked places were made straight and the rough ways smooth. See, John actually destroyed a type of 'false foundation'. If John didn't do this work then Jesus, the true foundation, wouldn't have been able to lay correctly upon the hearts of man or upon the region because a foundation can't be built upon an unlevelled surface.

God gave me this dream years ago to make me aware of what He was doing in a particular city. Forerunners were scattered throughout the city and since their unique message of revival wasn't yet fully embraced by the church, they served by teaching the church to observe.

Four years after having this dream, Holy Spirit spoke to me and told me there would be a tornado which would hit this particular city in the summer of 2011 and that not a single person would be harmed by it. He told me that it was being sent as a sign and wonder for the city. I was intrigued to receive this word since there hadn't been record of a tornado in this city since the early 1970's.

The small tornado hit the city in the summer of 2011 and not a single person was harmed. When I heard the news, Holy Spirit spoke to me and said, *"The forerunners who once stood outside of the church, have taught the church to observe the kingdom of heaven. As the church has observed, false foundations have begun to shake and crack. These forerunners are now going to be embraced by the church to train and equip the body to help re-establish the true foundation of Christ."*

Although this was what God showed me concerning the church of this particular city's state of growth, I believe this is an accurate picture of the season in which the global church is entering. I believe God has been using forerunners to break apart false foundations which our doctrines have been build upon, and now He is reshaping our theology to fit who Jesus the foundation truly is.

This needs to be important to us, because one of the things which will separate a mature forerunner from an undeveloped forerunner is how much of the foundation of Christ is engraved within the revelation they have received. Since revelation has so much influence on us, we need to always test it with God's character. We need to test all revelation we receive with the foundational truths in the Word of God.

This also needs to be important to us because as leaders in God's kingdom we need to live our lives from an accurate perspective of who Jesus is. He is the rock on which our lives need to be built upon. Where all of us are called to comprehend the foundation of Christ, some forerunners will be risen up to re-establish Jesus the foundation back within the church. These forerunners will re-establish the foundation by reintroducing who Jesus truly is to the church, thus bringing the body into greater alignment with the Head. Jesus the great apostle laid Himself down as the foundation for the broken.

At times we have tried to build our primary doctrines around Paul's epistles, when Paul said himself in 1 Corinthians 3:11 that no other foundation can anyone lay than that which is laid, which is Christ Jesus. Jesus is the foundation! If Jesus is the foundation, then we need to look at what He taught in order to understand the pivotal truths of the gospel.

I believe that throughout Jesus' life, His ministry pointed primarily to four pillars of truth, which I call the four corners of the true foundation. Jesus taught about the end of the law, which is grace. He taught about the kingdom of heaven, the Father, and He lived a life which exemplified the family of God. I have to laugh sometimes; people will come to me saying that I am unveiling new truths from the Word of God by teaching on things like prophetic encounters or how to move in the miraculous. Really, I'm just trying to point the church back to the foundation of Christianity. I'm just teaching the simplicity of the gospel because we've forgotten important elementary truths. I'm pointing back to grace, the kingdom, the Father and family of God because we can't build a proper spiritual house if our foundation is cracked.

We are going to walk through the four corners of the true foundation together to gain clarity and understanding as to what our lives should be exemplifying as a result of knowing Christ. Understand that some of this teaching may contradict what you believe or live out from your current revelatory standpoint. Ever since we were born into this world, culture and society has tried to teach us to think a certain way. God's heart is to reshape the way we think, to think like sons and daughters. This takes time. Be open to God messing up some of your theologies if need be. At times as the church we have allowed culture and society to mentor us by engraving man's thoughts into our view of the foundation of Christ, thus tainting our perception of it. Allow God to remove any substance of falseness. The only way for us to steward weighty pillars of ministry and influence is if we can allow God to complete His foundation within us. In order to reign as mature forerunners of Christ, we need to allow our hunger to lead us into the deep revelatory truths of Jesus.

Grace

Grace is one of the most pivotal truth's that marks the shift which happened through the cross. Even though grace is one of most potent truths of the cross, it is still one of the biggest stumbling blocks to people since it debunks the world's way of thinking. A lot of the church is still trying to interpret the Word of God through the lens of an Old Covenant way of thinking because grace is still misunderstood. This is why there has been a plague of the law's principals woven into our New Testament doctrine. If we are going to learn how to receive legitimate revelation from the Word of God then we need to learn to differentiate the Old Covenant from the New Covenant.

To be righteous simply means that you are in right standing with God. The Old Covenant was a contract between God and mankind which made man's standing with God dependant on how well he performed. Man's righteousness was the by-product of good acts

51

instead of identity. The Old Contract was a ladder formula to get to God.

Exodus 19:5-8: "'Now therefore, if you will indeed obey My voice and keep My covenant, then you shall be a special treasure to Me above all people; for all the earth is Mine. And you shall be to Me a kingdom of priests and a holy nation. These are the words which you shall speak to the children of Israel.' So Moses came and called for the elders of the people, and laid before them all these words which the Lord commanded him. Then all the people answered together and said, 'All that the Lord has spoken we will do.' So Moses brought back the words of the people to the Lord."

In verse 10 it goes on to say, "Then the Lord said to Moses, 'Go to the people and consecrate them today and tomorrow, and let them wash their clothes.'" God had the Israelites wash their clothes as a prophetic sign, showing that under the Old Covenant, how well we performed externally determined how clean we were.

See, the Old Testament was about cleaning up externally through works; where the New Covenant is about being transformed and cleansed from the inside out.

Since man couldn't complete the law to attain righteousness, God became a man so that He could complete the law for us. Since Jesus completed the law flawlessly through His works, we can receive right standing with God through the cross. This is why Jesus didn't stand at the right hand of God; He sat down because the work was finished. This is incredible news because it means that your closeness to God isn't dependent on what you do, it's based on what Jesus has already accomplished. We now live under a covenant of grace instead of law. In the Old Testament, Moses turned water into blood portraying how we lived under the ministry of death; whereas in the New Testament, Jesus turned water into wine as a statement that we have shifted into a covenant of life and celebration.

Shifting Covenant Lenses

The shift that took place between covenants is crucial for us to understand because we will read the scriptures through whichever lens of revelation we carry. Even Jesus' teachings can be interpreted in different ways depending on which perspective you look at them.

Read through some of Jesus' teaching from the sermon on the mount with me:

Matthew 5:17-30: *"Do not think that I came to destroy the Law or the Prophets. I did not come to destroy but to fulfill. For assuredly, I say to you, till heaven and earth pass away, one jot or one tittle will by no means* *pass from the law till all is fulfilled. Whoever therefore breaks one of the least of these commandments, and teaches men so, shall be called least in the kingdom of heaven; but whoever does and teaches them, he shall be called great in the kingdom of heaven. For I say to you, that unless your righteousness exceeds the righteousness of the scribes and Pharisees, you will by no means enter the kingdom of heaven."*

"You have heard that it was said to those of old, 'You shall not murder, and whoever murders will be in danger of the judgment.' But I say to you that whoever is angry with his brother without a cause shall be in danger of the judgment. And whoever says to his brother, 'Raca!' shall be in danger of the council. But whoever says, 'You fool!' shall be in danger of hell fire. Therefore if you bring your gift to the altar, and there remember that your brother has something against you, leave your gift there before the altar, and go your way. First be reconciled to your brother, and then come and offer your gift. Agree with your adversary quickly, while you are on the way with him, lest your adversary deliver you to the judge, the judge hand you over to the officer, and you be thrown into prison. Assuredly, I say to you, you will by no means get out of there till you have paid the last penny."

"You have heard that it was said to those of old, 'You shall not commit adultery.' But I say to you that whoever looks at a woman to lust for her has already committed adultery with her in his heart. If your right eye causes you to sin, pluck it out and cast it from you; for it is more profitable for you that one of your

members perish, than for your whole body to be cast into hell. And if your right hand causes you to sin, cut it off and cast it from you; for it is more profitable for you that one of your members perish, than for your whole body to be cast into hell."

If we were to try and interpret Jesus' sermon on the mount through an Old Covenant mindset, it could be read in a way where we could miss what He wanted to say entirely. If we read this through an Old Covenant lens, it looks like Jesus is saying, 'by any means necessary, don't sin, even if that means cutting off your hands and plucking out your eyes.' In fact, I've heard my fair share of pastors teach this very thing. If this was actually what Jesus meant then we would have a lot of limbless and eyeless people in churches. When we can perceive this teaching in what I believe it's intended context was, it seems as though Jesus is actually saying something completely different. Jesus was stating a point. He was creating a line of division between law and grace.

The word 'sin' translated from Greek means 'to miss the mark'. So, if you have a large target with a little red dot in the middle of it, and you shoot an arrow and hit the board even a quarter of an inch off the red dot, you have sinned and missed the mark. Jesus was saying that sin is sin. Whether you hit an inch away or three feet away, you've still missed the mark. Read this again, *"You have heard that it was said to those of old, 'You shall not murder, and whoever murders will be in danger of the judgment.' But I say to you that whoever is angry with his brother without a cause shall be in danger of the judgment."* The Pharisees thought they were living flawlessly because they weren't murdering, but Jesus was saying that even ungodly anger was the same thing because they were still missing the mark.

Look at what Jesus said, *"I say to you that whoever looks at a woman to lust for her has already committed adultery with her in his heart. If your right eye causes you to sin, pluck it out and cast it from you; for it is more profitable for you that one of your members perish, than for your whole body to be cast into hell."* Jesus wasn't literally telling people to disfigure themselves. I also don't believe that this was a teaching on how to keep pure by eliminating temptations. I believe that Jesus was throwing out a ridiculous scenario as though to say, 'So you want to be righteous through your works eh? Why don't you pluck out your eye so that it's impossible for you to lust after women?' Jesus was making a point saying, 'Apart from Me it is impossible for you to walk in righteousness through your works. You actually need Me to complete the law for you. You need grace through the cross.'

Jesus was making the same point when He said in Matthew 5:20, *"For I say to you, that unless your righteousness exceeds the righteousness of the Scribes and Pharisees, you will by no means enter the kingdom of heaven."* Jesus wasn't saying that your works need to be greater than the Pharisees in order to enter the kingdom; your righteousness needs to be greater. Jesus was bringing us to the end of ourselves by showing us that we need Him to complete the law on our behalf.

Look at this. Matthew 7:21-23: *"Not everyone who says to Me, Lord, Lord, shall enter the kingdom of heaven but he who does the will of My Father in heaven. Many will say to Me in that day, Lord, Lord, have we not prophesied in Your name, and done many wonders in Your name? And then I will declare to them, I never knew you; depart from Me, you who practice lawlessness."*

I've had countless people come up to me trying to use what Jesus said here to try and persuade me into believing that prophecy and miracles weren't for the present times we live in. Really they are just reading the scriptures through the lens of bad doctrine. In this teaching Jesus was showing us that at the cross there was a shift in covenants. The people in this teaching were clearly from New Testament times because they were moving in the prophetic and in wonders of God. Even though they were living in the New Testament they were still trying to present to Jesus all of their works by saying, *"Lord, Lord, have we not prophesied in Your name, and done many wonders in Your name?"* They thought that their striving would be an access to knowing Him. Jesus then says to them, *"I never knew you; depart from Me."* Jesus was saying that they completely missed the whole point of the cross and therefore didn't even know Him. He was saying that if we still try to live in a mindset of the law in New Testament times, we are telling Him that the cross wasn't good enough and that our works are a better bridge than His sacrifice.

I could come at this from hundreds of different angles. I'll throw a little eschatological curve ball at you just to mix things up. Have you ever wondered what the mark of the beast 666 means in Revelation 13:18? Six in prophetic numerology is the number of man, since man was created on the sixth day. There are three sixes. Three is the prophetic number of the Trinity. So the number 666 is a symbolic number of man trying to play the role of God. Where was the mark placed on those who followed the beast? It was placed on their foreheads and on their hands. This is symbolic of man trying to play the role of God by living in a 'Old Covenant mindset' by still trying to attain righteousness through the 'works of their hands', thus undoing the works of the cross.

It's good news that God made the Sabbath on the seventh day, showing us that Jesus died for a complete rest. He put to death our sinful nature, eliminating the temptation to ever have to rely on our own works. You are righteous (in right standing with God) through Jesus' works, not your own. Paul even said in Romans 7:17, *"But now, it is no longer I who do it, but sin that dwells in me."* Paul was showing us that our sin is completely separate from us through the cross. Our sinful nature was put to death.

Don't get me wrong with what I'm saying right now. I'm not saying that we should just go on sinning; in fact I believe there were many times throughout Jesus' ministry where He was actually raising the bar for Christians. He raised the bar for us because we are capable of conquering and withstanding temptations through grace. Grace covers us with the blood of Jesus, and enables us to live like He did. What I am saying, is we don't have to try living blameless for right standing with God. We live blameless because it testifies to who Christ is. Grace permits us to stand before the living God just the way we are, to be revealed into His direct image. We can reflect His image of blamelessness because grace empowers us to do the impossible.

Ministering From Grace

Grace is an extremely important revelation for the church to grasp in these days. I've met many forerunners who in their zeal would go about bringing great change in the world by bridging the kingdom to earth, but since they didn't know how to discern the Old Testament from the New Testament, their revelation became tainted and ended up causing more harm than good. When we live in an Old Covenant mindset, we will reflect the law in everything we do. If I don't understand grace in my relationship with God, then I won't extend grace in my relationships with people. Someone who doesn't understand grace will always judge people for their external works instead of honouring the internal man. Apart from grace we become too busy trying to show people their sins instead of loving on them for who God has created them to be.

We need to understand that our ministerial expression has changed because we live under a New Covenant. In the Old Testament, a common saying was, *"you shall love your neighbour and hate your enemy"* (Matthew 5:43). This was a common saying because in the Old Testament, whoever was an enemy of Israel was an enemy of God and vice-versa. This is why we could rejoice when David had slain Goliath. This is also why we could rejoice when the 400 prophets of Baal were killed through Elijah's ministry. Under the Old Covenant, since it was a covenant of death, we were used as vessels of God's judgement. It was a covenant where it was acceptable to love your neighbour and hate your enemy.

There was a beautiful shift that happened at the cross. In the Old Testament since we were under the covenant of judgement, we ministered in the ministry of judgement. Now look at what 2 Corinthians 5:18 says, *"Now all things are of God, who has reconciled us to Himself through Jesus Christ, and has given us the ministry of reconciliation."* This is a brilliant revelation which we need to grasp. Since the ministry of judgment has ended, we need to walk in our new ministerial role. Since we have been reconciled to the Father, our job is to function under the anointing of the ministry of reconciliation to reconcile the brokenhearted to the Father.

A lack of grace in the church has resulted in the church lovelessly trying to save the world. We are living in times where the world is violently trying to shape culture and society. Homosexuality threatens to pervert the sanctity of marriage, but this battle will never be won by angry Christians who don't know how to honour or love people. When we have a personal revelation of grace, we can honour by separating people from their disfunction, whatever it may be. I don't condone homosexuality in any way. I believe in taking social stands for what is morally right. As a minister I would never submit to legitimizing union between two people of the same sex. However I love homosexuals with all of my heart and I would give my life for any person who lives this form of lifestyle. In fact, I have very good friends who have embraced this way of life. Grace gives us the ability to separate sin from any individual. We don't have to agree with or support sin, but we need to allow grace to empower us to love and walk in relationship with people. Love and acceptance is what brings freedom, not a scolding fist.

The same can be said of abortion. I believe that abortion is a modern day Holocaust and the church needs to take a stand against this genocide. In the first and second century after Christ's ascension there was a terrible move of abortion. After giving birth, if parents didn't want their children they would just throw infants into different piles of garbage which were scattered throughout the land. Christians of that time had such a value for the human life, that they would intentionally dig through mounds of garbage to find children who had been abandoned. The Christians would then adopt the child into their families and raise it as their own.

Drastic measures need to be taken by the church to end this travesty, and I believe that one of these measures is to stop pretending that there isn't a problem. I heard a story from the times of the Holocaust in 1941-1945 of a church who met on a Sunday morning in Germany. The congregation began to worship, when they suddenly heard a train going by filled with Jewish people who were being taken to a concentration camp. Those who were in the train were screaming and crying out of a fear of losing their families and their lives. The church members instead of praying or taking a stand just increased the volume of their music because they felt that the cries were disrupting their service.

Just as Jesus took a stand for life, we also need to stand for the victims of abortion. This is a battle which needs to be fought with grace and love, not with condemnation. The only way to reshape the wrongs which have taken place is through kingdom love.

If any person reading this struggles with homosexuality or has had an abortion at any point in your life, I release you from feeling any form of guilt or shame. Jesus put an end to torment on the cross. I declare joy and peace into you right now. God's promise over your life is freedom and restoration. You are forgiven, loved and adored by your Father God. God loves you just the way you are.

Matthew 4:17 says, *"Repent for the kingdom of heaven is at hand."* When Jesus said this He wasn't saying "*turn or sburn!*" Jesus was saying, *"Change the way you think because there is a greater way of life available for you."* John 3:17, *"For God did not send His Son into the world to condemn the world but that the world through Him might be saved."* We need to wake up; we aren't living in the times of Old anymore. We aren't called to wait for Goliaths to come knocking on our doors anymore so we can slay them. We aren't called to be vessels of God's judgement. Instead we are called to chase down the Goliaths of the earth. We are called to chase down the pimps and drug dealers, not to condemn, but instead to be vessels of reconciliation by reconciling them to the Father!

If we are constantly stumbling over other peoples dysfunctions and aren't able to love with honour, then there is a good chance we are lacking a revelation of personal grace. I invite you to lay down your works. You're not received by God because of what you do; you are received because of who you are. The Father looks at you through the lens of the blood of the Lamb. You are blameless and perfect. The work has already been done. You don't have to stand before God's throne waving your works in His face. Take a seat on the throne with Him. Lay down the heavy burden of striving. Pick up the light yoke of rest.

The Kingdom

Throughout Jesus' ministry a vast amount of His teachings were about the kingdom of heaven. Since I covered a lot of ground in my first book concerning the kingdom, I am going to take a small excerpt out of 'Reigning As Royalty' to bring definition to the kingdom:

"We will start off in Luke 11:2-4. Tradition tells us that this is the Lord's prayer, however it is important to note that Jesus wasn't even praying; He was instead teaching His disciples how they ought to pray. When Jesus' disciples came to ask Him how they should talk to the Father He spoke and said; 'When you pray, say: Our Father in heaven, Hallowed be thy name. Your kingdom come. Your will be done on earth as it is in heaven.' The word 'kingdom' that Jesus referred to here literally means 'kings domain'. If the kingdom is God's domain, then we know that wherever the kingdom of heaven is, that's where God is - it is His dwelling place. The culture of a household is always a reflection of the culture or personality of the One who has headship over it. Since

God is heaven's creator, He is the head and authority of heaven which is His house. God in His very being is goodness and love. If heaven was God's expression in creation, we can be sure that its culture is a direct reflection of who God is."

"Look back at what Jesus says in verse 2; 'On earth as it is in heaven.' Jesus was literally telling His disciples to pray that whatever was going on in heaven would be made manifest on earth. Jesus came to release a revelation that it was God's heart desire for the perfection of the culture of heaven to co-exist with creation on earth. Many of us have gotten off track in Jesus' true Kingdom message. A lot of us are living to see and experience heaven one day when we die, when it was Jesus' desire for us to experience the blessings of heaven now while we are still on earth. Ephesians 1:3 says; 'Blessed be the God and Father of our Lord Jesus Christ, who has blessed us with every spiritual blessing in the heavenly places in Christ.' This doesn't say that He will 'eventually' bless us with every spiritual blessing in heaven, it says He already has. He said 'repent for the kingdom of heaven is at hand' (Matthew 4:17) saying that it is an attainable and tangible kingdom in hand's grasp. Heaven is in hand's grasp! This is good news! Jesus came to establish on earth a heavenly kingdom which functions out of heavenly principals here and now in our lives."

"What are some principles of heaven? We know that the Bible says that in heaven there is no sickness, no disease, no depression, addictions or poverty. There is only perfect love, perfect health, peace, joy and

abundant blessing. The kingdom of heaven is a place where God's will has complete rule and reign. When we receive Jesus as King we come under the rule and principals of His kingdom. We actually become citizens of heaven (Philippians 3:20). Sickness and addictions have no authority over us because they don't even exist in the kingdom that we are from. The Bible talks about two kingdoms; the kingdom of heaven (which is the kingdom of God) and the kingdom of darkness. When two kingdoms collide the greater kingdom will always prevail. A good example would be, say, if the kingdom of darkness had rule in an area of someone's life where they struggled with something like depression. When they receive Jesus as King in this area of their heart, His kingdom comes which is filled with perfect joy. Since God's kingdom is greater than the kingdom of darkness, His kingdom casts away depression, and joy becomes established in the individual's life."

- Reigning As Royalty

Power And Authority

It is our mandate as Christians to establish the kingdom of heaven on the earth. As a generation who is forerunning the second coming of Christ, we are about to discover tremendous potential that has been preserved for the last day church. I believe there is an increase of understanding concerning the revelation of the kingdom which transcends power, authority and even dominion, into the realm of ruling and reigning with Jesus. As forerunners we are about to tap into something that is going to turn the world right-side-up.

Many Christians walk in power, some walk in authority, fewer walk in dominion, but I have only met a few who know how to rule and reign.

I got the opportunity a while back to speak at a small youth group in the Caribbean. I was excited to speak to this particular group since many of the teenagers were troubled and had severe addictions.

For those of you who have done public speaking before, you'll know that usually while you are speaking you can discern how much faith and expectancy is in the room. Now, when I got up and grabbed the microphone let me tell you, the expectancy in the room was minimal, if not, non-existent. I made a sad attempt at trying to diffuse some of the tension by letting loose a few jokes. Hearing my sad puns plummet to the ground, I looked up to meet blank stares and was instantly acquainted with an awkwardness that was uncomfortably confrontational.

There was no momentum at all in the spirit, so I needed to create my own. I said, *"God just showed me that there's someone in the room who has pain on the outer side of their right foot. If you stand up right now, God is going to heal you."*

Instantly the youth pastor stood up and the pinched nerve in his right foot unpinched. All of a sudden the youth were attentive. I said to them, *"My heart isn't that you leave this place thinking that I'm a great man of God. Instead, my heart is that you will leave here believing that you yourselves are powerful and important people in God's kingdom."*

I began to create an atmosphere for the miraculous to occur. I shared a few testimonies of marketplace miracles and laid hands on a few youth for healing to increase the level of faith in the room. Since I could tell they were beginning to believe, I took everything a step further. Instead of continuing to lay hands on the youth to see them healed, I began to teach them how to move in the miraculous. One after another we saw all of these teenagers activated to perform miracles. They began laying hands on one another and saw Jesus healing through their own hands.

This is the difference between power and authority. I moved in authority by creating momentum that wasn't there. Those in the youth group moved in power by riding the momentum I created through authority. Do you see the difference? This is why many Christians walk in power but only some walk in authority. Some have the faith to create a wave where others only know how to ride one.

Bringing heaven to earth through authority has everything to do with knowing who you are in God's kingdom. Jesus said that the kingdom of heaven is within us (Luke 17:21), showing that we are actually carriers of the perfect culture of heaven. You are a powerful person. I remember a time when I was visiting a church that a friend of mine pastored. I was walking throughout the building checking the place out, when I saw a group of people yelling and screaming. I looked closer and saw that the group was gathered around a woman who was laying down on a mat. One of the women who recognized me ran over and started explaining to me the situation. She told me that the woman who was being prayed over had been a paralytic for nine years and that she had to bring a mat around with her everywhere she went. The woman continued to tell me that the group had been praying over her for an extended amount of time, and that they hadn't seen any breakthrough.

I walked over to the woman who laid on the mat and saw that she was frantic because of everyone yelling, screaming and rebuking demons around her. I told everyone who was there to stop shouting and praying. I sat down on the ground with this woman, grabbed her hand and whispered to her, *"You know, this can be a lot easier then all of these people are making it out to be."* I helped her up off of her mat and her body completely straightened out. She was healed and set free in an instant.

Dominion

Now, where many walk in power, and some walk in authority; fewer walk in dominion. We recently put up a prophetic booth at a city-wide festival. We started to notice that when we got to the festival that at times we didn't even have to pray for people to be healed. People would just walk up to the booth and the pain would leave their bodies. We have had times in our ministry where psychics who were trying to do readings around us would get aggravated because the kingdom that we released was cutting off their spiritual links so that they couldn't tell fortunes.

Where authority is creating the momentum and power is riding it, to move in dominion is to dominate the kingdom of darkness with the kingdom of heaven everywhere you go. Moving in revival has everything to do with how deep we allow the revelation of identity to sink. Peter walked in dominion to the extent where his shadow would just cast upon people and they were healed. In our ministry we have been learning how to cultivate a culture of dominion. There have been numerous times now when I have run up to someone on the streets to pray for them, and the person would tell me that all of the pain in their body left when I got a certain vicinity away.

Ruling And Reigning

As exciting as all of this is, there is still a greater aspect of governance that we carry in the kingdom of God. It stretches beyond power, authority and even dominion, into the realm of ruling and reigning. Check this out:

Revelation 2:26-27: *"And he who overcomes, and keeps my works until the end, to him I will give power over the nations - He shall rule them with a rod of iron; they shall be dashed to pieces like the potters vessels - as I also have received from My Father."*

Now, this is where things get really exciting! If you translate the words 'rod of iron' in this passage from both the Greek and Hebrew, it is translated to the same word which was used for the rod Moses carried. Moses, with the rod he carried moved in power, authority and dominion by performing signs and wonders before Pharaoh; but he also did something greater. With the ruling and reigning authority which was given to him from God, he actually had the power to deliver an entire nation. With the rod, he was able to take the entire nation of Israel out of the bondage and ideologies of the Egyptians.

We need to mature in the revelation of who we are in the kingdom. Some of us are still stuck having a hard time believing that Jesus still heals through His church, when God wants us to believe that we carry the power to deliver entire nations. We need to understand that we aren't just citizens of the kingdom; we are kings and queens of the kingdom (Revelation 1:6). We inherit the nations with Jesus and are called to rule and reign over them with Him because we were given the iron sceptre of royalty.

Moses was born in a time where there was genocide taking place. Pharaoh issued the abortion of every Israeli male babe out of a fear of the Israelites over populating the Egyptians. A woman in this era gave birth to a son, and hid him to preserve his life. After she could no longer hide him, she placed him in a basket and sent him down the river. The child's sister stood far off to see what would happen to her brother. Pharaoh's daughter went to the river to bathe and found the child. Having compassion on him, she called the sister over and ordered her to find a woman she could hire to wean the child. When the child grew, he was brought to Pharaoh's daughter and became her son. She named him Moses. From this point on, Moses was raised as the grandson of Pharaoh, the ruler of Egypt. Moses was learned in the ways of royalty. I believe that one of the reasons why Moses was able to deliver and lead a nation with such fluidity was because of his revelation of royalty to reign.

Maria Woodworth-Etter was a woman who moved powerfully in dominion. She would walk into a meeting to speak and people would experience notable miracles all throughout the entire stadium. As she would speak the Word of God, people would fall into visions of heaven which would lead to their salvation. As impressive as her revelation of dominion was, she was a woman who had a true revelation of how to co-rule and co-reign with Jesus. When Maria would speak at a meeting, not only would people in the meeting receive freedom, but something would actually shift within the region where she spoke. There are numerous accounts of crime rates dropping significantly within entire cities when she would release the kingdom within a church meeting. There are also many documented miracles that are recorded of people being healed simply because they were in the same city as Maria when she spoke.

Revelation 5:6: *"And I looked, and behold, in the midst of the throne and of the four living creatures, and in the midst of the elders, stood a Lamb as though it had been slain, having seven horns and seven eyes, which are the seven Spirits of God sent out into all the earth."*

Have you ever wondered why Jesus, the Lamb, had seven horns and seven eyes? Remember, the number seven in prophetic numerology is the number of completion. A horn in scripture is symbolic of authority. Since there were seven horns, this speaks of Jesus' complete authority over the nations. The seven eyes are symbolic of Jesus' complete wisdom and revelation to steward the nations (Ephesians 1:17-18). Jesus not only has complete authority over the nations, but He also has complete wisdom and revelation in how to steward them. This is why He is entrusted to open the scroll which is the strategy of God. We get the great privilege of partnering with Jesus in His governance over the earth.

Kings And Queens Of Creation

Psalm 2:7-8: *"I will declare the decree: The Lord has said to Me, 'You are My Son, today I have begotten You. Ask of Me, and I will give You the nations for Your inheritance, and the ends of the earth for Your possession.'"*

One time when I was standing before the Lord in an encounter, He told me to close my eyes and to stretch out my hands because He had a present for me. I closed my eyes and held out my hands, when I suddenly felt the bulk of an object press into my palms. My eyes opened to see what the Lord had given me. To my surprise, I saw that I was holding a small city. He then shared with me that I was transitioning into a season where I would learn how to co-reign with Him.

Jesus said to me, *"The first principal you need to understand to co-reign with Me is that whichever land I have called you to, is land you have inherited."*

As forerunners of the kingdom of heaven we are called to establish the order of heaven in whichever land we are called to, whether that's a city, school, business, workplace or family. Wherever we are called, it is our responsibility to bring kingdom invasion. A forerunner will prepare the way and level out the land so that Jesus can dwell as sustained revival. We are by no means ever to be on the defence, but are always on the offence forcefully advancing the Father's will. Jesus would bridge heaven to earth by puppeting what was going on in heaven (John 5:19-20). Everywhere the sole of His foot would touch, the kingdom would take reign in that land. Since Jesus was the King of the kingdom, He would actually inherit wherever the kingdom was established since the kingdom of God holds greater authority than the kingdom of the world.

Joshua 1:3: *"Every place that the sole of your foot will tread upon I have given you."*

Revelation 4:4 is probably one of the most profound verses in the Bible concerning our royal standing: *"Around the throne were twenty-four thrones, and on the thrones I saw twenty-four elders sitting, clothed in white robes; and they had crowns of gold on their heads."*

The number 24 is the number of heavenly government, because it marks the 12 tribes of Israel and the 12 disciples who were the governing authorities of the early church. Through the cross we are seated on thrones around the King of kings, given golden crowns of authority to reign with Him. We rest as the highest ascendancy of heaven and earth under God.

Genesis 1:26: *"Let Us make man in Our image, according to Our likeness; let them have dominion over the fish of the sea, over the birds of the air, and over* *the cattle, over all the earth and over every creeping thing that creeps on the earth."*

When God made mankind in His image, He had given him all authority over creation. Since Adam and Eve were the governing authority, all of creation was under subject and submission to the king and queen of creation.

Galatians 4:3: *"Even so, when we were children, were in bondage under the elements of the world."*

This verse talks about how when we were children (still under a mindset of the law) we didn't carry complete authority over the elements of the world. When we come to a revelation of royalty to reign, we actually walk in an understanding that we rule over the elements of creation just as Adam and Eve once did before the fall of man. The actual Greek definition of the word 'element' is 'the elements from which all things have come, the material causes of the universe'. The elements this verse is referring to are technically the elements of the periodic table, since they are the substance of everything material. You actually carry such governing authority over the nations to the extent where you can command the very elements the nations are created from!

Haven't you ever wondered how Jesus could walk on water and command fig trees to wither? Or why Paul wasn't harmed when he was bitten by a poisonous snake in Acts 28:3-6? Jesus could walk on water because H2O had to submit to Him by doing whatever He commanded it. Paul could remain unharmed after being bitten by a poisonous snake because he actually reigned over the elements which poison is created from. See, there's a depth to your identity that exhibits kingship or queenship over the nations. You are a king or queen of creation.

I do ministry in Ottawa, Ontario from time to time. Right before I left for one of my trips from Calgary to Ottawa, Holy Spirit told me that He wanted to teach me about my reigning authority over creation. He told me that when I would leave from Calgary to Ottawa or vice-versa, the exact same weather in my departing city would manifest in my arriving city the very moment I crossed the provincial border.

I quickly went on the internet to see what the contrast in weather was between the two cities. Calgary was at a steady -31 and was experiencing an extreme blizzard, where Ottawa was at a mild -9.

I hopped on the plane and went to Ottawa. The second the airplane crossed the border into Ottawa I watched snow begin to fall as I peered out the window. Within 10 seconds the exact blizzard that was in Calgary manifested in Ottawa. The pilot then came on the intercom saying that Ottawa's temperature drastically decreased and now stood at a steady -31 degrees.

Time and time again, I have seen creation respond when I jump between cities and nations because creation will always live up to par with the sons and daughters of the living God.

Reigning Over Cities And Nations

Adam and Eve, as a king and queen over creation were immune from any form of sickness, disease, pain, addiction, or emotional turmoil. Since they had authority over the land, all of creation had to live up to the standard of life which Adam and Eve lived. So, just as man was free from all spiritual, emotional and physical bondages, the land in turn followed man's lead by living in a free state, immune from things such as deadly-natural disasters, famines and plagues. Creation will always live at par with the son.

When the fall of man occurred, Adam and Eve gave up their right to immortality and became vulnerable to the things they were once immune from. Since the land was under submission to man, it actually didn't have a choice but to follow him into his lower standard of life, making itself also vulnerable and subject to wounding. The baton of governance on the earth was then placed upon the shoulder of the enemy (Luke 4:5-6). Although an authority to reign was passed, we can consistently see a thread throughout the Old Testament of creation responding to the actions of mankind.

In 2 Samuel 21 it talks about how there was a famine which broke loose throughout Israel. King David went to inquire of the Lord concerning why a famine was taking place. God answered David saying, *"It is because of Saul and his blood thirsty house, because he killed the Gibeonites."*

The Gibeonites are mentioned in Joshua 9 as a tribe who dwelled outside of Israel. Israel, without consulting with the Lord had come into covenant with the Gibeonites vowing that they wouldn't kill them. A peace covenant was made before God between the Israelites and the Gibeonites which lasted many years. When Saul took kingship over Israel, out of zeal for Israel and Judah, he killed the Gibeonites, breaking the covenant between men before God. Since covenant was broken between men, the wrath of God was poured out which actually brought a wounding to the land, invoking a famine. See, the land could only live up to the standard of life which mankind lived up to. It wasn't until David went and made peace with the Gibeonites that the land came to a place of being restored and the famine ceased.

In Genesis 4, it talks about how two brothers named Cain and Abel were presenting their offerings before the Lord. God could see the motives of the brothers' hearts and was pleased by Abel's offering but not with Cain's. Cain became jealous and killed his brother, making Abel the first martyr recorded in human history. God then spoke to Cain in verse 10 and said, *"What have you done? The voice of your brother's blood cries out to Me from the ground."* See, since Cain made the decision to live below the standard of life that God called him to live, it didn't just effect God, his brother, his family or even himself. When Cain stumbled it actually defiled the land and brought it further from it's God-intended state.

The original commission of man was to expand the kingdom beyond the garden into the nations, to discover, uncover and reveal the identity of the land. Every town, island, tribe, city, province, state and nation has its own purpose and function in stewarding revival. Instead of setting a good example for the land to follow, by not living out our sonship and daughtership, we have instructed creation to live in suffering. Now that authority again rests upon the shoulder of the Son (Isaiah 9:6-7), in New Testament times all that it takes for the land to be brought into restoration is for sons and daughters to stand in their God-given identity. When creation sees us as forerunners living life from a kingdom mindset, creation can't help but live up to the same standard of life.

In Genesis 32, Jacob is travelling to a piece of land called Jabbok. The Hebrew meaning of the name 'Jacob' is 'supplanter'. *Jabbok* translated from the Hebrew language means 'emptying'. Jabbok was a place where the filth of the land was emptied into from a river. So Jacob (supplanter) goes to a place called Jabbok (emptying) and comes into an encounter with God where he wrestles with Him through the whole night. Jacob was so changed by this face to face encounter with God that his identity was completely rewritten. Where before his name defined his character, Jacob came into a new revelation of his standing with God, so God actually renamed him. Jacob, now known as Israel which means 'God prevails', was a new man with a new purpose and identity. Israel came to the conclusion that since God showed up in such power, that even the land he was in couldn't continue to walk in the same identity it once did after encountering the living God. So, Israel renamed the land naming it *Peniel* which in Hebrew means 'facing God'. The destiny of the land which was once to be a place where filth was emptied, transformed to be a place which would represent the beauty of God all because a man took a step forward into his God-intended state.

Whenever God shows up and we begin to receive a greater understanding of our sonship or daughtership, we live life at a higher standard which gives the land permission to rise to her greater potential. This is why Paul said in Romans 8:19 that *"For the earnest expectation of the creation eagerly waits for the revealing of the sons."* Creation is groaning and waiting in eager expectation for sons and daughters to be revealed, because it still remembers what it was like when it walked in wholeness back in the Garden of Eden days. Creation still remembers what it felt like to be whole. Jesus was the first Son to be revealed and ever since the cross and resurrection more sons and daughters are rising in understanding of their identities. In Joel 2, Joel was prophesying about a great army that would be risen up, the likes that the world had never before seen. This army is a prophetic picture of the last day church which is being risen up to destroy the works of the enemy and to restore creation. Whenever we are brought to greater revelation of our royalty, the land rejoices because the kings and queens of creation are restoring things to how they once were.

Joel 3:2: *"the land is like the Garden of Eden before them."*

The word 'intercede' in Hebrew means 'to meet', so intercession can be as easy as meeting with God and encountering Him on behalf of our families, cities and nations. When we do this we bridge the gap between God and creation. This means that in every prayer or worship meeting, as we begin to walk in a fuller revelation of who we are, we aren't the only ones experiencing a change. Something in the land actually comes to a place of wholeness. When we see God encounter someone in a hospital by seeing them healed, yes, they are healed and changed. Yes we are encouraged by seeing God move. But, we need to understand that since a son or daughter was revealed, the DNA of the hospital begins to come into alignment with heaven. I am convinced that if we start making the choice to position ourselves to constantly encounter Jesus we will see businesses, restaurants, schools and entire cities transformed.

Remember what happened when God encountered both Moses and Joshua (Exodus 3, Joshua 5). They were instructed to take off their shoes because they were walking on holy ground. Moses and Joshua were actually getting to experience creation in the way God had originally intended it, because the land began to be brought to wholeness. I believe when Moses and Joshua took off their shoes as they stood on holy ground, that this was a foreshadowed act of man coming into a reconciled relationship with the land. It was a prophetic sign that mankind would take his rightful stand to rule and reign over the nations.

A few years ago I went through a 10 day season where I would encounter the power of the Lord at night in a very extreme way. God's power would come so strongly that I would be woken up because my bed would physically shake.

After the tenth night that this happened, I asked the Lord why He was shaking my bed. He then began to speak to me about Revelation 22:2 which says, *"In the middle of its street, and on either side of the river, was the tree of life, which bore twelve fruits, each tree yielding its fruit every month. The leaves of the tree were for the healing of the nations."* He began to talk to me about how in order for people to get to the tree of life to grab the leaves which would bring healing to the nations, that they first need to walk through the garden of intimacy with Him to get there. There is no other way to carry an authority to bring true healing to the nations other than through true intimacy with God.   He then said that He was shaking my bed because beds are a prophetic symbol of intimacy.

Obviously I couldn't sleep after this, so I decided to go for a walk. When I arrived back home after my walk, I was about to enter my bedroom when the Lord spoke to me again saying, *"Remember, you need to walk through the garden with Me intimately in order to get the leaves of the tree of life which bring healing to the nations."* I opened my door and saw that there were about 20 physical leaves scattered across my bed.

I truly believe that we are in a time in the church globally where we are beginning to grasp a firm hold of intimacy with the Lord. We have been learning about the friendship of God on a greater level and have been understanding how to worship Him as He sits on His throne. I believe that we are now entering a season where God wants to release the leaves of the tree of life over different individuals, ministries and churches. Where before the church walked primarily in a priestly anointing which is an anointing of intimacy and worship, now the priestly anointing is being bound to a kingly anointing, because through the cross we were made both kings and priests (Revelation 1:6). Since this is what is taking place, Jesus is going to be training His bride to not only worship Him as He sits on His throne, but also to teach her how to sit on the throne to reign with Him.

Revelation 3:21: *"To him who overcomes I will grant to sit with Me on My throne, as I also overcame and sat down with My Father on His throne."*

God is training us to understand that since Jesus overcame, so have we because we have overcome by the blood of the lamb and the word of our testimony (Revelation 12:11). Therefore, we get to sit with Him, to reign with Him on His throne. We are coming to a time in history where revivals and moves of God aren't just going to impact singular churches or communities. We are actually going to see entire cities transformed into the likeness of the kingdom of heaven. Just as in the Old Testament, there were entire towns and cities which reflected hell, such as Sodom and Gomorrah; in New Testament times, we are about to see entire cities completely set apart for the things of God. There will be cities where disease can't even exist within their district. I believe addictions will fall right off of people when they come in the vicinity of specific regions. Cities will actually walk in dominion by dominating the kingdom of darkness, because the saints will understand their place of royalty to reign over them. It all begins with sons and daughters being revealed. It begins with a revelation of the kingdom which inhabits us and longs to be released. It begins with us learning how to pick up our iron sceptres of royalty to rule and reign with Jesus.

Take up your sceptre. God has called you to deliver a nation.

The Father

The Father Reveals The Son

I meet a lot of people who have tremendous zeal and desire to be released into ministry prematurely. You can actually tell very easily if someone is ready to be released into platform ministry or not. You can tell by observing whether or not they carry the qualities of a son or daughter. Everyone wants to be a spiritual father or mother, but you will never be a good spiritual parent until you can first learn to be a son or daughter.

John 20:16-17: *"Jesus said to her, 'Mary!' She turned and said to Him, 'Rabboni!' (which is to say, Teacher). Jesus said to her, 'do not cling to Me, for I have not yet ascended to My Father; but go to my brethren and say to them, 'I am ascending to My Father and your Father, and to My God and your God.'"*

Jesus portrayed someone who intimately walked with His Father God. He was so intimate with His Father to the point where His whole ministry was the reflection of His Father's heart (John 5:19-20). I could soak in this one verse for hours. Jesus said, *"I am ascending to My Father and your Father."* Jesus shows us that because of the cross, God was no longer just Jesus' Father, but He is also my Father. He is also your Father. The cross gave us grace so we are in right standing with the Father, permitting us to have an intimate relationship with Him.

True sons and daughters always find themselves in the Father. This is why the revelation of the Father is so important. It's important because it is actually impossible to know who we are apart from Him. Without Him our lives are plagued by identity crisis.

In Daniel 1, the prophet Daniel and his four friends Hananiah, Mishael and Azariah were brought into king Nebuchadnezzar's service. While entering their training to serve the king, they were given new names. Daniel (which means God is my judge) was called Belteshazzar (meaning lord of the straitened's treasure). Hananiah was named Shadrach; to Mishael was given the name Meshach; and to Azariah, Abednego. This was actually a brainwashing technique. Nebuchadnezzar tried to take away their names which glorified God, to give them new names which instead glorified his own gods. He was trying to trick them into believing they were someone who they were not. He was trying to rewrite their identities.

We live in a world where right when we are birthed into material existence, society tries to tell us who we are. The lies of the world try to mask our identity by placing titles and trends upon us as an attempt to hide who we truly are. It tries to categorize us and stick us in the "appropriate" forums. This is why many of us live life not knowing who we are.

Revelation concerning your identity is found within the secret place of intimacy with the Father; nowhere else. This is important for any young leader to know. Your most profound training for ministry won't be behind a microphone; it will be in the cave. It will be in the face to face encounters you have with God. It's in this place where the world's assumptions of who you are, begin to burn away revealing who you were truly created to be.

Right as I began school, my teachers noticed that I learned differently than the other children. Those who taught me assumed I had learning disabilities and enrolled me in special help classes. I felt as though I was being placed in the category of being stupid. This of course wasn't true. However, when you're told by people who you look up to that you don't learn well, you will quickly take on that trait as part of your identity.

It's fascinating how we dismiss what we don't understand. Uniqueness which was meant to be a gift becomes quenched until it is completely snuffed out. Genius is a common component of every person's identity; we just dismiss it because it often doesn't fit into our forum of comfort.

After embracing this false label, I immediately stopped trying to do well in school. When my teachers would begin teaching the class I would automatically tune out because I assumed that I wasn't smart enough to understand what they were going to say. This false perception of who I was followed me through all my years of education. In a few of my classes in high school I stood at a steady 14%. Throughout my 12 years of schooling I had actually never finished a book because I tricked myself into believing I couldn't understand what I read.

By the grace of God I somehow graduated high school. A few years after I finished my schooling, I distinctly remember the Father speaking to me through an encounter.

I was walking with the Father throughout a library in heaven when He led me to a section of books. As I pulled one of the books off of the shelf, He began to tell me that these books were letters which were set aside for the last-day church. I looked at the book's cover and saw my name where the author's name was usually written. The Father then spoke to me and said, *"Luc, you've always believed you were stupid; but I'm going to show you how brilliant I've created you to be."*

From this point on every time I would begin to feel as though I couldn't achieve something as an intellectual, I would start speaking over myself that I was brilliant. I did this because I wanted to receive the new name my Father was trying to give me. He took my false identity and gave me a new one. He burned away the chaff of all of my teacher's curses and unveiled hope and purpose.

When the Father spoke this truth into me and broke me out of category by revealing my sonship, I successfully finished the first book I ever read; the Bible. Shortly after this I began writing my first book. It was a challenge to write to say the least. It would take me about 45 minutes to focus my thoughts enough to write a single sentence. Yet, since I knew what the Lord spoke to me, I continued to write. After hours upon hours of work, I wrote the first 50 pages of my book. To be honest with you, when I reread what I wrote it sounded like absolute gibberish. But the Lord then spoke to me and told me to begin rewriting my entire book. As I did, writing became natural. I could actually formulate my thoughts and compose proper sentences. In the span of 45 minutes instead of only writing a single sentence I could write pages. Since I was able to receive what my Father said about me, I was able to break out of a false identity which before that point I had embraced for my entire life. Now I have the great privilege of impacting the masses as an author.

Honouring The Process Of Creation

We try to pull all sorts of teachings from Genesis 32 when Jacob wrestled with God. To be honest with you, I don't think that this was as much of a teaching about a man's persistence, as it was about a man who didn't fully comprehend how to receive blessing. I don't think that it was God's heart to wrestle with Jacob; His heart was to bless him. God's main purpose for encountering Jacob was to change his name. Remember, 'Jacob' in the Hebrew means 'heel holder' and 'supplanter'. The English definition of supplant means to 'scheme'. God came to Jacob with the intention of changing his name from 'Schemer', to Israel which means 'God prevails'. Jacob, out of stubbornness tried to hold onto an identity that was below the standard which God called Him to live, therefore wrestled with God.

We live in this constant tension of God teaching us to think from the perspective of a son or daughter. We often live day-to-day wearing false labels as an identity until God speaks the truth by trying to reveal who we truly are. Instead of believing what He says about us, we often end up wrestling with God by trying to hold onto our false identities. We do this because we find comfort in familiarity, and even though the lies we have embraced about ourselves hurt us, they are familiar nonetheless. We fear stepping into freedom because we understand bondage. We are masters at adapting to it because we have lived in it our entire lives. Embracing truth means admitting we have been wrong about ourselves. Pursuing freedom comes at a cost of admitting that God knows us better than we ourselves do. Once we put aside our stubbornness we can begin to allow God to train us to live life from our true identity.

This is a good word for many of you to receive. It's good because I can guarantee that a lot of you reading right now are incredibly introspective without even realizing why you are. To be introspective in moderation isn't a bad thing. However, extreme introspectiveness can be a form of wrestling with God in order to keep our false identities. Here's a classic scenario: Have you ever walked into a room of people and instantly feared you wouldn't fit in? There are three different responses we can have in this type of situation:

This first response is the correct course to take. We can make the decision to stand in the uniqueness of who God has created us to be. Instead of submitting to a fear of rejection, we can confidently stand in who we are, permitting our individuality to influence the culture.

The second option is that we shut down and willingly submit to the sidelines of community. When we do this we have already made the decision that we will be rejected so therefore don't step out to be received. We actually forfeit our individuality in these moments by masking our personality with isolation. This reaction to community will always lead to extreme introspectiveness because we feel different and desire to understand our indifference.

Lastly, we can respond by submitting to feeling on the outside of what is taking place, so therefore adapt to our surroundings by altering our individuality in order to be received. Instead of confidently standing in our uniqueness, we often compromise our rarity out of a fear of being misunderstood. This course will always result in becoming unnecessarily reflective and introspective. We become reflective because we have subconsciously rejected ourselves by attempting to be someone who we are not.

I'm going to give you an extremely good key concerning breaking out of extreme introspectiveness. Here it is; we become introspective because we feel as though we need to over-analyze our internal man in order to understand ourselves. Understanding your identity has very little to do with how good you are at analyzing yourself. It has everything to do with how much you trust the One who created you to tell you who He has created you to be. It has everything to do with how much you trust the Father to reveal your sonship or daughtership. It isn't your responsibility to over-analyze yourself. You don't have to live a life of trial and error in an attempt to understand who you are. The reason is this; you have a Father who knows exactly who you are. Instead of spending hours wrestling through self-analysis, ask the Father who knows everything about you. If you step into a room and begin to fear rejection, ask the Father who you are. Stand in the uniqueness of what He says about you. When we can stand confident in our uniqueness, then we don't acclimatize to other cultures; we shift and influence them.

We are in a constant state of God creating and forming Jesus the Son within us.

Genesis 1:2: *"The earth was without form, and void; and darkness was on the face of the deep. And the Spirit of God was hovering over the face of the waters."*

The words 'without form' in Genesis 1:2 come from the Hebrew word *tohuw* which means 'place of chaos'. This is interesting to me because even though there was chaos, it was a part of creation which God said was good (Genesis 1:4). God saw the conflict as good because it was part of the process of creation. When we encounter situations where we feel confused about who we are, we need to understand that even though our inner hurts could be surfacing, this is a part of God creating something which He deems as good. This is part of the Father forming the Son within you. God lives in this place of conflict, tension and chaos. He will surface a lie so that He can rename us; thus teaching us to live from the perspective of sonship and daughtership.

Blessed are the pure in heart for they will see the face of God. People will usually relate purity to children, when in my opinion, children better portray innocence. Purity is created through conflict just as iron sharpens iron. Even if you look at the process of gem stones being created, they obtain their purity through immense heat and pressure. As we grow older throughout our journey with Jesus, we should essentially be seeing through the lens of purity more and more. As we grow into understanding our purity through refining, we will begin to see the face of God continually. Blessed are the pure at heart.

A Letter To Forerunners

Let me state something, I'm not saying that righteousness is a process because I believe that we were made righteous through the cross. What I am saying, is that even though we are righteous and pure, there is sometimes a journey in re-patterning our mind to think from a righteous and pure perspective. Righteousness is instant, but renewing your mind is a process.

I had an encounter a while back where I was standing before the throne of God. Jesus immaculately sat upon His throne, portraying a size which reflected a mountain. I grabbed the train of His robe and began to climb. I eventually climbed my way to God's head and was able to pull myself up onto His crown. I walked slowly across the brim of His crown looking at the gemstones which ornamented it. I came across a large blue gemstone in which I could see my reflection. Looking at the gemstone, I saw that in my reflection I was clothed with the royal linens of a king. I took my eyes off of the stone and looked down to see myself wearing a ratty garment. Holy Spirit then spoke to me and said, *"Stop dreaming about the man you want to be and step into your royalty to be the man I've created you to be!"*

I stepped forward, plunging into the gemstone's purity to be clothed as the king that I am.

It's time for us to give up to the Father. We need to stop trying to hold onto our false identities. Receive the fire of God that burns away the assumptions of what

96

the world has expected of you. Forsake the false identity that your teachers have tried to speak over you. Abandon the false labels that your family, friends or enemies have placed upon you. Stop wrestling and receive your name.

If you look at the 12 tribes of Israel, it symbolically portrays a very accurate historical timeline of the church. We are the Benjamin generation who was the last son born of Israel. The most remarkable thing which separates Benjamin from his older brothers is that every other son of Israel was named by their mother. Benjamin was the only son named by Israel his father. Past generations of the church have in many ways been named by society, culture and their mother, the church. But, this Benjamin generation is tapping into a beautiful revelation of the Father. The Benjamin generation is the generation who is willing to embrace the names their Father has chosen for them.

The world will try to categorize you, but it's time to break out of who the world expects you to be. Stand in your uniqueness, because in your uniqueness you present an aspect of the image of God which no one else can display. God has ordained you to release an aspect of the Father's heart which no one else can present. No one has ever lived a life like you live with Jesus. You don't have to live co-dependently, basing your worth on what others think of you. You also don't have to live independently as though you need to guard who you are or what you carry from others. You can actually live interdependently, knowing fully who you are, and coexisting with others without swaying in your identity. Be yourself. Embrace your true self. Let your genius shine and point the nations to your brilliant Creator.

A Mantle To Father

Understanding our sonship is essential to maximizing our impact through kingdom expansion. Encountering the Father teaches orphans that they are sons and daughters; then teaches sons and daughters to be fathers and mothers. Although our righteousness was bought through the cross, how close we are in relationship to the Father is up to us. Some minister on the earth, trying to move heaven by speaking to the Father as though He is a far off deity. Others who understand their heavenly citizenship apart from sonship stand in the throne room gazing upon God from a distance as though He isn't relational. Those who truly understand they are sons and daughters become one with the Father. As He sits upon His throne, they sit on His lap and lay their head on His chest. They minister from this place. Taking notice to what His heart beats for, they allow the melody of their hearts to harmonize. This is where sons and daughters become fathers and mothers. These are the ones who will father and mother the nations, parenting entire regions to transform into the likeness of the kingdom of heaven.

Back in Bible times, it was Jewish custom for a father to take his son on as his apprentice to train him in whichever trade the father worked as a profession. Once the son reached the age of 30, he would then step out of his father's apprenticeship to work as the head of his trade. Jesus being Jewish kept with this Jewish tradition. Jesus was under mentorship to God the Father His whole life. He learned what the Father's heart broke for. At the age of 30 when Jesus was baptized, the Father spoke and said, *"This is My beloved Son, in whom I am well pleased"* (Matthew 3:17). Note that the Father acknowledged that Jesus was living from a place of sonship in this verse. Right after His baptism, Jesus was led to the desert for 40 days and then was immediately released into ministry to do the work of His Father. See, Jesus went from being fathered, to being a Father of the disciples and Israel. This transition always needs to take place in order for us to maximize kingdom influence through our lives. It's important for us to understand that even though there is a transition into mothering and fathering, we forever remain sons and daughters.

A few years after I met Jesus, I was brought into an extensive season where God had confronted many lies I believed about myself with truth. This was when God drew a clear definitive line showing me that I was a son instead of an orphan.

I was partnering with a church at the time which was experiencing a fresh move of God. There was a pastor at the church whose name was Jim Redner. Jim is still one of the most fatherly men I have ever met. As I ventured to the end of this vast season of inner healing I was walking to the Sunday morning service. On my way, Holy Spirit said to me, *"Jim Redner is going to give you a mantle of fathering today."* Unsure as to what God meant, I tucked the prophetic word in my pocket and kept on my way.

I arrived at church and the service started. Sitting on the front pew I began pursuing my Father's heart in worship. Suddenly I could feel someone's eyes on me. I looked to my left and saw Jim sitting next to me. Jim looked at me while wearing a blue blazer which complimented his fatherly smile. He stood up, took off his blue mantle and placed it upon my shoulders.

There is a new fathering and mothering mantle being released over the church in this day. We need to understand that this mantle of fathering and mothering can only be stewarded well when we know that we are primarily sons and daughters. Not only will your greatest training be found in your encounters with your Father, but your most profound expression of ministry will come from this place. Your most profound expression will come out of this place because you begin to receive a father's heart.

Have you noticed how when you hear specific people teach there is weight to their words? This is because they are speaking with authority. When Jesus would teach, this was what separated Him from the scribes (Matthew 7:29). Jesus could teach with authority because He experienced everything He taught. If we want to speak with authority, we need to stop teaching only what others are teaching and start teaching what God has already taught us. We need to speak from the place of encounter. See, it's in this place of direct relationship where we will see our greatest fruit. You are only an encounter away from changing the world.

St. John's greatest revelation and message to the church was in his exile on the island of Patmos. The book of Revelation was conceived through a radical heavenly encounter which John had with God. God knew that John understood his sonship and stood as a father to the early church, so therefore could be entrusted with such an important message. If we truly want to see the world changed then we need to make the decision to encounter the Father's heart.

The Power Of Legacy

A while back I was heading to the funeral of a personal role model of mine who I knew briefly before his passing, Robert Cochrane. Robert was an amazing husband, pastor, father and stepfather of two girls; one of whom is my wife. The funeral was five hours outside of the city, so I left at 5:00am to get there in time. Since my wife was out of town, I drove alone. After about an hour of driving, staying awake became an immediate challenge. I was trying my hardest to not fall asleep, when I was suddenly made alert as I saw with my peripheral vision the form of someone sitting in my passenger seat.

I looked to my right, and saw a man next to me wearing the finest of linens and a glorious yet modest crown. Unlike when I encountered John the Baptist who was ratted and covered in dirt, King David looked immaculate. David gazed through the front window of the car with tears brimming his eyes. He projected a humility which I don't think I have ever felt coming from anyone in the whole of my life. He was a man whose greatest desire and greatest delight was to serve the Lord. David began to speak, although, when he spoke, he spoke in Hebrew. At times while speaking he would laugh with joy. At other times he would weep. He did this for the total of two and a half hours.

While listening to David, I asked God to interpret the Hebrew tongue for me. Holy Spirit responded by saying, *"If you will study David's life for the next four months then I will interpret his tongue through his life story."*

Holy Spirit then said, *"During the eulogy of the funeral, I will give you a key which will begin to unlock the revelation I want to reveal to you through this encounter."*

At the funeral I listened intently during the eulogy. I heard Robert's testimony; the testimony of a man who served Christ with all of his heart. This man had such a profound walk with God where his anointing actually began to echo into the latter generations of his family. Bob's influence wasn't just to those he himself pastored. But, he was able to parent the anointing he carried into his children. I listened to how every one of his children diligently serves God and how four of the seven have stepped into pastoral ministry or are married to a pastor. Many of his grandchildren also entered into full time ministry as the by-product of his life. Bob was able to develop his mantle, anointing and giftings as a five-fold teacher and pastor throughout the generations. While listening to this man's testimony, I received an incredible key to the kingdom which began to unlock what God wanted to teach me; legacy.

I kept the concept of legacy in mind as I studied David's life for the next four months. The thing that fascinated me more than anything about David was how he constantly took the generations into consideration. As David would live his life, he would record his internal processing and prayers through the Psalms. He did this firstly, as an act of intimacy with God. King David's Psalms were songs he wrote from the depths of his heart to God. The Psalms are an intimate conversation between a man and his Creator. Secondly, the Psalms were written as a method of leaving legacy. Through David's times of suffering, he would journal. Through his times of victory and joy, he would journal. Since David did this, it allows everyone who reads his writings to learn what David learned from God without having to experience the circumstances he went through to learn them. David's experiential wisdom which he left behind can actually become basic grounds of logic for anyone who is teachable enough to receive it into their spirit. To this day people flip to the Psalms when they are in distress or trouble. These songs have pastored and counselled people for generations, because true intimacy with the Father develops a father's heart to leave legacy. David did incredible work for the kingdom while he was on the earth, but because he understood the wisdom in creating legacy through the Psalms he continues to advance it even after his death.

At the end of my four months of study, I was sitting in a coffee shop when I fell into an encounter. I sat at the table as I got to audibly re-listen to what David said when he visited me in my car four months earlier. Not a laugh or cry was taken out from what he said. The only difference was that when he spoke, he spoke in English instead of Hebrew. I originally thought David was speaking forth a teaching. However, for the full two and a half hours, I listened while David shared testimonies of different people throughout the course of history who had been transformed through the legacy of the Psalms. He laughed and wept his way through sharing each beautiful story.

True fathers and mothers will always take the upcoming generations into consideration. In the Old Testament, it was custom for a father at the end of his life to lay his right hand on the firstborn son to impart blessing (Genesis 48). This was done so that the works of the father's life would live on throughout the generations. Many people consider the book of Numbers to be pointless unless you dig deep into historical genealogy. However, Numbers is a consensus showing numerous accounts of how many were influenced by a single person. The book of Numbers is a historical log of legacy.

John the Baptist was an incredible role model as one who walked as a forerunner from a place of integrity. Before Jesus' ministry began, John was the spearhead to what God was revealing to mankind. He was the talk of Israel. Look at what this great minister says in Mark 1:7, *"There comes One after me who is greater than I, whose sandal strap I am not worthy to stoop down and loose."* At that time, even though John was the primary vessel for what God was doing, he would prophesy that One greater was coming whose anointing would surpass his own. He shows his father's heart by declaring that the next generation minister would have greater impact than he himself did. When Jesus arrived on the ministry scene, John even allowed one of his own disciples to follow Jesus because he knew that Jesus could bring his former disciple to a greater place of spiritual maturity then he himself could. This level of fathering can only take place when we come to understand that our life is about building God's kingdom instead of our own. Jesus had the same heart; He said to His disciples whom He fathered, *"Most assuredly, I say to you, he who believes in Me, the works that I will do he will do also; and greater works than these he will do, because I go to My Father"* (John 14:12).

While David was older in years, the king's servants would bless him to comfort him by saying, *"May God make the name of Solomon better than your name, and may he make his throne greater than your throne"* (1 Kings 1:47).

This is the heart every forerunner needs to have to see lasting fruit through their lives. We need to believe that those who we father and mother will have greater impact and influence than we have ever dreamed of for ourselves. Whenever I speak at a church, Holy Spirit tells me to believe that every single person listening to me speak will go on to have a greater ministry than I myself do. We shouldn't have to become disciplinary to develop this heart for those who we pour into; this wisdom for kingdom expansion is the direct by-product of someone who holds firm to humility. Humility is always the fruit of someone who consistently encounters God in His greatness. It is a father's pleasure to see his children live better and more purposeful lives.

Matthew 27:24-25: *"When Pilot said that he could not prevail at all; but rather that a tumult was rising, he took water and washed his hands before the multitude, saying, 'I am innocent of the blood of this just Person (Jesus). You see to it.' And all the people answered and said, 'His blood be on us and on our children.'"* The blood of Jesus left such a powerful legacy where it echo's throughout the generations. The same Spirit which empowered the work of Christ to ride throughout the generations dwells in you, meaning that as you co-labour with Jesus, it is God's will that your work will create legacy.

God has called you to leave a legacy. Your legacy is the children who you leave behind, whether your children are parented through relational fathering or mothering, or by monumental substance that can live beyond your days. Don't cut the world short by hoarding anointing, wisdom and platform. Build your anointing for the purpose of duplicating it in others. Create platform to give it away. If you have worked to excellence in any area, leave visible footprints for others to walk in so they don't have to rebuild before they can start where you left off. Allow your children to stand on your shoulders to reach new dimensions in heaven so that the generations after them can reap the harvest of your life. Teach on your failures as much as your successes, so that stepping over ditches you stumbled into become common grounds of logic for those who are teachable. Teaching from your mistakes demystifies your excellence, making it accessible to others. Your life is a parable full of treasure. Let people in. Allow them to live life with you relationally, just as Jesus did with His disciples. Let them dig through the vastness of your experience in day-to-day life.

The Family Of God

The Kingdom Is Built Upon Kingdom Relationships

Several years ago the Lord began to speak to me concerning a revival which was going to take place in a particular city. He said to me that this city had been pregnant with revival for many years and that for the next two years the city would be in labour to give birth to a great move of God. Holy Spirit showed me that the contractions from the labour will be the intercession of the church calling out to God to see heaven dwelling on earth.

We went through two years of very intentional intercession for this city and saw the birthing of revival which broke out that following year. Revival isn't true revival if it stays in the church. True revival extends beyond the four walls of the church and influences culture. Just as Mary took care of Jesus and nurtured Him when He was a newborn child, we had to learn to tap into a mothering anointing by nurturing a revival in its infancy stages. I went to the Lord to consult with Him on how we should go about maturing this infant revival, and what He said to me will echo throughout my soul for the rest of my life. He said to me:

"The only way the church will be able to properly raise and mature a newborn child is if the church can learn to be a family. A child can only grow healthily within community."

Since we are entering a new age where the forerunners of God are being revealed, there needs to be clarity concerning one of the most fundamental revelations of the gospel. In order for us to live a life where the diversity of God can be celebrated throughout His body, the uniqueness which every forerunner portrays needs to be embraced by the family of God. I honestly believe that the revelation of the church being a family is one of the most timely and important messages for the church to receive if we are to steward revival from a place of maturity. God's heart is for every individual to be birthed into a family instead of an orphanage.

God the Father sent His one and only Son to die on a cross so that He would have many sons and daughters. As soon as Jesus overcame sin and death, a royal family born of Spirit and Truth began to be birthed and multiplied throughout the nations. Wherever this family would tread their feet, more sons and daughters would be born into royalty. This revelation of the church being a family is one of the most profound truths which separates us from the rest of the world. It is also one of the key truths that will reunite heaven to earth binding them together in sustained revival. When the world can see that we love one another with a genuine love, and receive those who the world has branded as unlovable, the church no longer becomes a place to be feared or mocked. It becomes home.

I am married to a beautiful woman of God who grew up on a small island in the Caribbean called Bonaire. On our recent trip to Bonaire the Lord had me observing the wealth of culture in Bonaire in comparison to what we consider wealth in North America. Where in North America we hold incredible value to our independence, in Bonaire, people's wealth is found in their families. There are positives in living in a country that upholds independence. Culture has taught the North American church that it's important for us to understand our separate callings. It has taught us to know how we are called to function to edify the body of Christ, which is necessary in seeing the church reach maturity. However, after seeing a culture like I saw in Bonaire where everyone is loved as though they are family, makes me wonder if some of the North American church has submitted to a culture of independence to such an extreme that we've stepped into the deep end of individualism. This is where things get scary because when we walk only as individuals, we can never fully co-exist in the church as one family. If we are separate from the rest of the body, our personal dreams and visions begin to claim ground in front of our relationships which contradicts how Jesus set His priorities. Jesus shows us through His life that He put His relationship with His Father above all things. Second were His relationships with others, and then came ministry.

Jesus modeled how the church was supposed to be a family instead of a non-relational institution throughout His entire ministry. In John 17, Jesus prays His final recorded prayer and begins to talk to the Father about how He had been faithful with what was given to Him. It's interesting to me that Jesus doesn't mention the things that a lot of us would likely mention while talking about our successes. Jesus didn't talk to the Father about how He was in a spotlight ministry where the masses would follow Him day and night. He didn't mention His healing ministry or how through His teaching ministry He unveiled mysteries which hadn't been discovered since the foundations of the earth were made. He didn't even bring up how He lived a life separate from sin. Instead, Jesus shows us where His true priorities laid. He talked to the Father about how He was faithful with the twelve disciples who were given to Him. Even though Jesus was used as the catalyst that sparked a revival which redirected history, He shows us that His main focus and mandate was to be committed in relationship with those the Father had given Him. Since Jesus' priorities were in order, the move of God would go without fail because revival can only be sustained if it's built upon a network of proper friendships and relationships.

I am a blessed man to have the family and friends God has given me. The people who I consider true friends alongside of me in ministry are the ones who ask me how my family is before they ask me about how well my ministry is doing. Years back I was preparing to walk along side of a church that was bringing me in to develop a prophetic outreach ministry in their church. I was very young in ministry and to be honest with you I hardly had a clue at all in what I was doing at the time. One day while I was resting with the Father preparing my heart, He spoke to me wisdom that rerouted my understanding of the church. He said to me, *"Luc, if you want to see this ministry succeed you don't need to focus as much on the gifts of the Spirit as you do on how to walk in proper relationships. If you train and equip the masses to prophesy and heal the sick you will be doing a great work for the kingdom's cause, but if you learn to be a good friend then you will see the nations transformed."*

When Holy Spirit told me this it instantly shifted my understanding of where my priorities should be. I understood that being faithful with the few relationships God gave me before the masses was not only God's order, but I also learned that stewarding the masses properly was actually the by-product of being in close transparent relationships. This is a very crucial revelation for anyone who is called to be a leader in the church. You can't reverse God's order of priorities because each priority functions to sow into the following. Our relationships with people can't be put above our relationship with God because it's our relationship with Him that teaches us to walk in Godly friendships. Since this is the case, when there is a flaw in how we walk in relationships, we know that it is just the by-product of something that hasn't come into full alignment in our relationship with our Father. It's the same with how our relationships are to stand before ministry. You will never learn to be a good friend, husband, wife, father or mother through what you learn in doing ministry. God made family before He made the five-fold ministry. It's being faithful in your relationships that train you to be a great leader to the body. Take time sowing into them. For too long, men of God have cheated on their families with ministry. If you are a man and are called as a leader in the church, whether you are an apostle, prophet, evangelist, teacher, pastor, worship leader, intercessor, whoever you are, how you treat Jesus' bride will always be a direct reflection of how you treat your own wife.

Take some time to read through Matthew 10:5-15: *"These twelve Jesus sent out and commanded them, saying: 'Do not go into the way of the Gentiles, and do not enter the city of the Samaritans. But rather go to the lost sheep of the house of Israel. And as you go, preach, saying, 'The kingdom of heaven is at hand.' Heal the sick, cleanse the lepers, raise the dead, cast out demons. Freely as you have received, freely give. Provide neither gold nor silver nor copper in your money belts. Nor bag for your journey, nor two tunics, nor sandals, nor staffs; for a worker is worthy of his food. Now whatever city or town you enter, inquire who in it is worthy, and stay there till you go out. And when you go into a household, greet it. If the household is worthy, let your peace come upon it. But if it is not worthy, let your peace return to you. And whoever will not receive you nor hear your words, when you return from that house or city, shake off the dust from your feet. Assuredly, I say to you, it will be more tolerable for the land of Sodom and Gomorrah in the day of judgment than for that city!'"*

Jesus was so strategic in the commissioning of His disciples. Notice how He sends them out to teach and manifest the kingdom but doesn't allow them to bring anything in the natural that would allow them to live life in the practical sense day by day. Instead of ordering them to bring money, or an extra pair of clothes, He tells them to go to the Israelites and to stay with them in their homes. While sending them to demonstrate the kingdom He was actually making it impossible for them to not walk in relationship with those they were ministering to. This was a profound teaching on commitment that Jesus taught His disciples. In the church of Acts we see that the believers didn't have one place where they would meet but they would meet in the houses of believers (Acts 20:20). These apostolic connections throughout Israel which we see in Acts were made when the disciples were first sent out at the great commission. Jesus the great Apostle brilliantly used His disciples to plant the first churches without them even knowing they did it! Jesus in His wisdom knew that even though the disciples were going out and demonstrating the kingdom, that revival could never be sustained unless it was built upon kingdom relationships.

John 19:26-27: *"When Jesus therefore saw His mother, and the disciple whom He loved standing by, He said to His mother, 'Woman, behold your son!' Then He said to His disciple, 'Behold your mother!'"*

The model of government that God has chosen for the church is family.

Forerunners Vs. Lone Rangers

Out of all four corners of the foundation, I believe that this final one is in many ways the most difficult truth to walk out healthily. The fact that fresh revelation marks a forerunner is an incredible blessing, yet it is a truth which needs to be understood with integrity. The revelation that no one has lived a life like you live is a wonderful privilege; yet it needs to be married to the understanding that your difference binds you closer to the family of God, not separates you.

Just as John the Baptist had to submit to a season of separation from Israel, many forerunners will feel as though they stand apart from the church in a revelatory state. I'm not saying they are called to walk independently from the body. I believe every believer needs to be woven into the church and should be under submission to pastoral council and under apostolic covering. What I am saying, is that there is an ordained time for a forerunner to stand apart (not stand alone) for a time to see a side of God that hasn't yet been revealed to the rest of the church. This is where our uniqueness can actually be a stumbling block to our understanding of the family of God if it isn't viewed through a healthy lens.

The body of Christ is the depiction of diversity. As forerunners of Christ we get to display undiscovered aspects of God's nature. When diversity is viewed through the lens of love, we become a people capable of the impossible because a more complete expression of who God is can be represented through unity. It is our diversity that equips the bride to partner with Jesus in binding heaven to earth. However when diversity is viewed through the lens of fear, we are quick to divide because we feel more safe partnering with those who are similar to us. There is a temptation to isolate out of a fear of our uniqueness not being celebrated. When we view the church's diversity through the lens of fear, we open a door for one of the most dangerous pitfalls towards forerunners. This is when the enemy will try to turn a forerunner into a lone ranger.

Just like all of you who are reading this book, I have had the privilege of walking in a forerunner call immediately when I was birthed into salvation. I'm going to share a bit of my own journey of growth concerning my understanding of the family of God as a tool to teach from.

A Letter To Forerunners

I was born and raised in Calgary AB, Canada in 1988. Growing up I was incredibly shy. I lived in a mindset where I was constantly paranoid of what people thought of me. Instead of living from a place of confidence, insecurity would control how I related to people. This held me back from knowing who I actually was in my personality. I fell victim to loneliness at a young age and due to a fear of rejection began to isolate myself. Out of a fear of the world, my bedroom became my safe place and refuge.

In my teen years, I began looking for love and affection from people. Since I didn't know what love looked like, I therefore didn't know where to look. I started drinking heavily at the age of 13 and became a sex addict at the age of 14.

I had a friend at the time that went to a Christian youth group. After a lot of persuading, she eventually convinced me to come out with her. I went to her small conservative church with the intention of being received by any means necessary. At this point in my life, I thought that being a Christian simply consisted of doing good things, so that's exactly what I did. I quit drinking, stopped having sex and pretended to be a Christian.

By my graduating year, I successfully played the role of a "Christian" for two years so well, that the leaders of the youth group made me one of the leaders. My role consisted of leading a small group of six male teens. I attempted to disciple them into knowing who Jesus was when I didn't even know Him myself. I am one of the few who can actually say that I was a church leader before I was a Christian!

One night while I was leading the group of guys, we began a group discussion concerning spiritual gifts. We went around from person to person, stating how we felt God had gifted us. There was a young man with us that night who I had only met a time or two before. When it came to his turn, he told us that he received the gift of tongues when he was baptized in the Holy Spirit. Since the church I was part of didn't mention Holy Spirit often, I was immediately intrigued. I said to the young man, *"Dude! I want to hear what tongues sounds like. You should do it for me."* Since I put him on the spot it took him about 15 minutes to build up the courage, but he eventually began walking around the group speaking in tongues as he laid his hands on each of us. The power of God slammed down, and all six of us guys were lying on the ground wailing uncontrollably for about three and a half hours. I was saved, baptized in the Holy Spirit and fell completely in love with Jesus all in this one night.

After experiencing the love of God in such a tangible way, I dove head first into Him and became obsessed with His presence. Every day after school or work I would come home, drop off my bag and head outside to walk with Jesus for four to six hours. When I would wake up on my days off, I wouldn't even turn on my light. I would just lay praying and spending time with God for eight to 12 hours before I even got out of bed. In this period of my life there were times when I would save up my money so I could take time off of work for four months at a time. On my time off I would soak with Jesus in His presence every day for about 14 hours. God began to develop my ears to hear His voice. I started having encounters where I could see what was going on in heaven before I even knew what a third-heaven encounter was. Obsession drove me into the

Word of God, even though at the time I hardly knew how to read.

Since the church I was attending at the time hadn't experienced many manifestations from Holy Spirit, how I encountered God was very misunderstood. Without me even realizing it, right from salvation my hunger to know God intimately commissioned me into being a forerunner of revival. All I had to do was say that I had a dream from God and gossip about me would spread throughout the church like wildfire. A few families felt they couldn't be part of that particular church anymore because they didn't want to be around people who supported the idea of God still speaking today. Not knowing what to do with me, out of frustration and panic, some of the leadership of the church began to take me aside to discredit me and label what I was experiencing as heresy. I was caught up in a shroud of persecution which came from the church, hardly understanding how my relationship with God sparked so much offense.

I remember one time distinctly about six months after I gave my heart to Jesus. I was coming back from a retreat with my youth group when we stopped at a coffee shop for a bathroom break. When I came out of the washroom I saw one of my leaders standing in a circle with a bunch of my peers. I walked over to join them until I began to hear what my leader was saying. I overheard him making my relationship with God the centre of his jokes. He was telling jokes about how I was insane and how I have lost my mind. Immediately I felt wounded after experiencing rejection by someone who I held in such high regard.

When I was home later that day I went into my room, sat down on the floor beside my bed and broke down crying out to Jesus. All of the persecution and rejection I had faced the previous six months caught up with me in that moment. I found it baffling how my love for Jesus was the birth of such controversy. Even though people were getting offended I knew I could never reject God's love for me because of persecution. He was everything to me.

Huddled beside my bed, I cried until I was too exhausted to stay awake. I crawled up into my bed and went to sleep. A few hours passed, when I was awoken by the presence of someone in my room. I was laying with my face towards the wall as I began to hear soft footsteps approaching me. At first I thought it was my brother trying to creep up on me, until I felt a gentle touch on my shoulder. This one touch was motivated by such pure acceptance that it dethroned any hurts from rejection in my heart. Jesus spoke audibly to me. He said, *"Luc, you can sleep for now. But, a time is coming when I will call you to stand as a prophet to the nations."* Jesus then began speaking to me different details concerning my calling. Dumbfounded by what was happening, all that I could do was lay in my bed sobbing. I didn't share this encounter with anyone for over six years.

Persecution from the church increased when I received my Father's compassion for the sick and I started stepping out in faith to see the miraculous. I stayed around the church that I was at because I didn't actually know that there were other Christians who heard God speak and were living to see heaven on earth through the expression of revival. I hadn't yet heard of the great revival schools or renewals that God was birthing throughout the nations. So, for the first three years of being saved I pursued the presence of God with everything I had completely ignorant to the fact that there were others who were hungry for a move of the Spirit.

As we pursue the deep things of God, we should be seeking out a network of people who support the word that God is depositing within us. Although this would obviously be the preferable choice, it isn't always the most realistic at times if supportive people are scarce. I know many forerunners, including myself that in their earlier years of learning to steward the revelation they received, had to stand by themselves in their understanding for a season. Thus is the cost at times of being a first fruit of revival. When we are in this place we can either stand with God, or stand alone. If we stand with Him in the secret place, we will complete our mandate in receiving the forerunner message and grow in our love for Jesus' bride. Whereas, if we stand apart from Him, we chance walking our season in loneliness and bitterness towards God and the church.

One of the greatest threats a forerunner will face is a mindset of independence. Every forerunner walks in an advanced revelation standing as the spearhead for what God wants to reveal to the church. Since they will at times stand a distance apart from the rest of the body in maturity, wisdom, understanding or zeal, the mindset that you are alone can easily creep up on you. Few have the stamina or courage to embrace such a call, but to those He has called, He has prepared in His strength. Few have the stamina or courage because it takes great confidence to stand unflinchingly in your identity when the world is aggressively confronting your personality with the prison of normality. As you forerun, the key you need to understand is that you receive the stamina and courage to persevere in His strength, not your own.

The primary step which needs to be taken in order to avoid the pitfall of extreme independence is rooting yourself in the secret place with the Father. This sounds like a basic statement, especially since we have already covered a lot of ground concerning the Father's heart. But, the truth is that often when an individual feels misunderstood because of his or her identity or gifts, their uniqueness which is meant to be a blessing can often feel like a curse. When this type of mindset is formed it can often lead to bitterness towards God. If we permit this stronghold, then bitterness can become an open heaven for loneliness to seep in.

There needs to be a clear understanding of identity for all forerunners that they are called as a gift to the church. This can only come when they find their true sonship and daughtership from the Father. When we are one with Him, we can't help but know that we are called to be part of something greater than ourselves. Whereas if there are walls that have been put up then it's easy to believe the lie that we are called to be alone, because we are different. It's our steadfastness in pursuing the Head that gives a forerunner hope to function in unity within the body.

A Message To The Prophetic Community

Although this section is more targeted towards those whose giftings gravitate to the prophetic ministry, know that this is applicable to everyone since we all carry the call of a forerunner to one extent or another.

Shortly after Jesus visited me in my bedroom, persecution started coming at me from different angles. My friends who I confided in started saying I was too heavenly minded for them and that they didn't want to be in relationship with me. A few people who I was very close with actually started planning on trying to commit me to a psych ward because I was saying that God still spoke and healed in these days.

Since I no longer had any support, I felt that I was getting too hurt trying to stand against my current church's constant criticisms. This was when I embraced one of the most dangerous lies a prophetic person can swallow. I believed that I would never be received, that I had no friends and that I was completely alone, other than my friendship with God. I left my church and embraced isolation. Persecution drove me from my past relationships and fear of rejection chained me from pursuing new ones. I went about a year and three months by myself where not only Jesus was my best friend, He was my only friend.

Understand that I'm not writing this to receive sympathy. I am writing because the reality is that there are many prophetic people and forerunners across the globe that live in similar circumstances and don't know how to cope. If we don't learn to live in our uniqueness from the perspective of victory, then we will end up not completing our mandate in expanding the church's understanding. Not only that, but we can also end up very wounded. I have met a lot of people who were trained and equipped in revival schools, but now that they are out of that environment, they are unsure of how to deal with being in a culture that rejects who they are.

One of the most dangerous pitfalls for a prophetic person is isolation. A wounded prophetic person will isolate because of a fear of being misunderstood and rejected. If a person is highly prophetic and feels as though God has "cursed" them by making them different, they can begin to walk in a pattern of thinking that assumes God will only ask them to do things that they don't want to do. This way of thinking can distort a forerunners view of God from seeing Him as a dictator instead of a Dad. They could even see isolation as a form of obedience to God, believing that their discomfort pleases Him. This false perception can often lead to rebellion and an unwillingness to submit to church leadership.

Often upcoming prophets or highly prophetic people in general will battle with feelings of loneliness or isolation because of the rejection that comes with the territory of the call. In fact, I've never met a person who has had a legitimate call as a prophet who hasn't experienced tremendous rejection. However, just because we are facing rejection, doesn't mean that we need to embrace a wound of rejection. We always get to decide whether we step over oncoming criticisms or catch them in our hearts, taking ownership for other peoples' dysfunctions and assumptions.

It can be a hard thing for a prophetic person to find his or her place within the church. It's in a prophet's DNA to be satisfied with nothing but the Lord Himself. Even when a prophet is in a group of people, it can be easy to feel alone since you are at times misunderstood because of the unique ways that God will speak to you. Even though your emotions may be telling you that you are alone, I can tell you in confidence that you are not. There is a Father who loves you, whose intent in gifting you the way that He has was not meant to be a burden, but a gift. You are part of a great royal family. Even if you haven't felt the embrace yet by the church, don't allow your heart to harden towards them. You are called and there is a place in the body that fits who you are perfectly. He has not ordained for you to be alone.

In a prophet's heritage traced back to the Old Testament, the prophets would be revered and set aside from those who would hear their words. They stood apart from their fellow man because of the disunity which separated man from one another ever since the tower of Babel. Many New Testament prophets or prophetic people have taken on the burden of their heritage assuming that the 'New' would be the same as the 'Old'. Fortunately this isn't the case. It is God's heart for prophets and prophetic people to be embraced by God's family just as everyone else is. You are fearfully and wonderfully made. No matter how different He seemed to have made you, He rejoices in your uniqueness because in that you bear His image in a special way that not many do.

Recently God has been giving me different keys and has been having me teach a lot on kingdom relationships. At first I was hesitant because I felt as though I was stepping beyond my prophetic office to do the work of a pastor. I consulted the Lord and asked Him what He was up to. He told me that since isolation is one of the most dangerous pitfalls for a prophetic person, that the revelation of the family of God is one of the most timely and most valuable messages that needs to be communicated to the prophetic community. God went as far as to say to me, *"A prophet isn't walking in maturity in his or her calling, unless they can model to the body of Christ that they walk in a healthy relationship with the family of God."*

Remember what Malachi 4:5-6 says: *"Behold, I will send you Elijah the prophet before the coming of the great and dreadful day of the Lord. And he will turn the hearts of the fathers to the children, and the hearts of the children to their fathers."*

The prophetic community has been on the sidelines of the body of Christ for years, but we are beginning to see a drastic change. This verse shows us that one of Elijah's jobs as a prophet in a New Testament time is to bring reconciliation to families. Not only is the prophetic community called to walk as one with the church in relationship, but they are also called to be part of training the church to be reconciled as a family. The prophetic community reconciles the church as a family by revealing the body's diversity in all of its callings, mantles, anointings, giftings, and talents. The prophetic ministry actually shows the church that it can't function properly apart from one another; but that every aspect of God through His church has precious value. The prophetic community won't be able to complete their mandate in the church, if it stands on the sidelines of the family. It's in relationship where the rest of the body will be able to trust the prophetic ministry to minister in this capacity. Great influence is the by-product of trust which has been built in relationships.

It can be an incredibly frustrating thing when as a prophetic leader you know that you are called to train and equip the church, but you are terrified that you will be rejected by her. The sooner that we can hand over to Jesus our fears and frustrations towards the church, the less that thoughts which say we are alone can creep up on us. Here is a timely word that any forerunner should take to heart:

Remember the story of Elijah (1 Kings 17-2 Kings 2). Elijah is a fascinating prophetic leader to me because even though he did extraordinary acts of faith, what is recorded of his life also shows common struggles that many of us face. Elijah did a great thing for Israel by killing the 400 prophets of Baal. Right after Elijah does this bold act, Jezebel threatens his life causing him to flee. Now in this moment of distress, Elijah begins to over exaggerate his circumstance. Elijah says in 1 Kings 19:14, *"I have been very zealous for the LORD God of hosts; because the children of Israel have forsaken Your covenant, torn down Your altars, and killed Your prophets with the sword. I alone am left; and they seek to take my life."* Elijah goes as far as to ask God to take his life (1 Kings 19:4). How many of you can relate to this? One moment you're standing in absolute faith, and then in the next moment you're slipping into self-pity and begin doubting yourself. One moment you are speaking the word of the Lord in faith, and the next moment you feel defeated and crushed due to persecution.

What God does to bring Elijah out of his depression touches my heart in a very profound way. God tells Elijah to go and appoint Elisha as a prophet to be the successor of Elijah's ministry. It isn't hard to see the closeness that Elijah and Elisha walked in. Whenever Elijah wanted to go and do a ministry task by himself, Elisha refused to leave his side (2 Kings 2:2-6). Elisha actually called Elijah 'father' because they were so close relationally (2 kings 2:12). Sometimes we assume that the solution to our problem will be difficult because our problem seems difficult. Elijah's solution was simple. He was in a place of distress, so God gave him a friend. Elijah was depressed, so God brought him into community.

Paul reiterates what happened to Elijah very well in Romans 11:3-5: *"Lord, they have killed Your prophets and torn down Your altars, and I alone am left, and they seek my life?' But what does the divine response say to him? 'I have reserved for Myself seven thousand men who have not bowed the knee to Baal.' Even so then, at this present time there is a remnant according to the election of grace.'"*

Even if you feel alone, take courage because you are not. God has risen up a remnant and we are drawing towards a time where the remnant will pull together as a great spearhead for revival. Since we know and prophesy in part (1 Corinthians 13:9), we can be confident that God won't raise up a single forerunner in a place without raising up numerous others to steward the whole vision. Although there may be a season where connections seem scarce, there is a time where God's elect will assemble. Through experience and time I have seen moves of God birth when the forerunners of a city begin to network together as the leaders of sustained revival.

A Home For The Lone Ranger

A risk in adopting a mindset of extreme independence is that it will obscure a person's mindset in how they view the church. If we take on the idea that God has destined us to walk a life of solitude because of who we are in Christ, we can begin to view the church as a stepping stone for our own callings. This is how ministry and self-mandate can take a stand before family and kingdom relationships which can very well lead to failure.

Joseph's life which is recorded in Genesis 30-50 is a good reflection of what it looks like to be a part of a non-relational institution instead of a family. While Joseph was living at home as a young child he was adored by his father. One night God spoke to Joseph through a dream telling him that he was to rule over his brothers. Out of zeal, Joseph told his brothers about his dream. His brothers became jealous and faked his death by selling him to a group of Egyptians. It's interesting to note that it was a manifestation of Joseph's prophetic call that first initiated his persecution, just as it is with many forerunners. After much trial, character development, and favour, Joseph finds himself as second in command over Egypt under Pharaoh. Because of his position, anything he wanted was at hands grasp. Any command that he made would instantly be established in the land by the authority which was given to him. He was at the top of an institution, yet there was a void which prevented true happiness from reigning within him.

At this time, there was a famine in Israel. Joseph's brothers came from their homeland to Egypt looking for food. Joseph's longing to belong in a family was evident due to his reaction to seeing his brothers. He would cry and wail after seeing them because he knew that family was his home, not his place in platform.

There is no unselfish support in an institution that isn't first founded out of family and relationships. They are filled with individuals climbing a corporate ladder, driven by a hunger to belong. The higher they climb, the more status becomes their pillar of identity until they realize that the spotlight is a lonely place when you stand alone. The life of a lone ranger should never be a lifestyle that is coveted. Loneliness isn't holiness, it is bondage and it is a life separate from true beauty. It's a simple thing to see Jesus in notable or creative miracles, but it takes someone who knows Jesus as a true best friend to see Him in relationships.

Matthew 18:11-13: *"For the Son of Man has come to save that which was lost. What do you think? If a man has a hundred sheep, and one of them goes astray, does he not leave the ninety-nine and go to the mountains to seek the one that is straying? And if he should find it, assuredly, I say to you, he rejoices more over that [sheep] than over the ninety-nine that did not go astray."*

God's heart is to free lone rangers from their shield of independence. Notice in this verse that the man is looking for a sheep and not a goat that wandered from the 99. In Jesus' parables He would often use sheep to symbolize believers and goats to symbolize non-believers because they don't know Jesus as Shepherd.

This is pivotal to understand because even though lone rangers are saved, they are separate from the rest of the flock because of a lack of revelation concerning Jesus the shepherding Pastor. Remember, a pastor's job in the body of Christ is to train and equip the church to be pastoral. So essentially, they train the body of Christ concerning relationships. Jesus' heart is to find every lone ranger who is lost in their own heart wounds and to lead them back to the family of God.

Stepping Out Of The Wilderness

For those who have fallen into a lone ranger mindset, there needs to be a clear distinction between a God-ordained wilderness season and a self-ordained wilderness season. God delivered Israel from Egypt through Moses; but, He expelled Egypt from the hearts of the Israelites through the wilderness. The purpose of the wilderness was to free the Israelites from the sin and ideologies that they received while being in Egypt. Most forerunners who have embraced the mindset of a lone ranger will go through some type of wilderness season. Wilderness seasons ordained for lone rangers are meant to remove a false independence from their hearts so that they can enter the Promised Land which is the family of God. Once this desire and commitment for true unity births within the forerunner's heart, the wilderness has done its job. However, as we all know, the amount of time spent in the wilderness is dependent on our willingness to let Holy Spirit work within us.

This is where the distinction between a God-ordained and a self-ordained wilderness needs to come in. God ordains a wilderness to bring us to the end of ourselves, where our self-ordination and stubbornness prolongs our stay. I don't believe it was God's initial will for the Israelites to be wandering the wilderness for 40 years. Estimation from different scholars present that the Israelites' journey should have taken anywhere from 11 to 30 days from Egypt to the Promised Land!

A young man walked up to me at church a while back. He had a very weighty prophetic calling, but in the past was very hurt by church leadership. He said to me, *"The Lord spoke to me last night and told me that He is commissioning me into a 15 year wilderness season where I am going to experience isolation and separation from the church."*

I told him, *"I should probably fill you in on something; God didn't speak that to you because He isn't the one who decides how long you are in the wilderness for. You do."*

When we lose hope in the church, the wilderness becomes a vast place. We need to honour Jesus' bride by seeing her the way that Jesus sees her, pure and spotless. When we perceive her through a hurt lens, we no longer desire to be part of her, making us wander without a destination. Time and time again, I've met forerunners who have lost hope for Jesus' bride. They assume that God has prolonged their stay in the wilderness when really they stay there by choice because they choose to live according to their hurts instead of by faith. Lone rangers try to run from their own heart issues throughout the wilderness and then blame God and people for the pain that their own stubbornness has created.

When Adam walked the earth, he would walk with God amongst creation observing the animals and their mates. He would look for a suitable helper that he could call his bride. God saw that it wasn't good for man to be alone, so He put Adam into a deep sleep, opened his side and took out one of his ribs. Adam's bride who was once a dream and a desire within him was taken out to be formed and fashioned. Thousands of years later Jesus hung on a cross and His side was split open just as Adam's was. Ever since this point in history, the bride of Christ has been in the process of being formed and fashioned. We need to understand that the church is still being formed and perfected to reflect the heart of God. As forerunners of today, we may get hurt and even rejected by the church at times. If she lives below the standard of life she is called to, that isn't an excuse for us to escape. We need to commit and see past her dysfunction into who she was created to be; the pure and spotless bride, the representative of the hope to the nations and the family of God.

Once I embraced the lie believing that I would always be alone, I wandered through the wilderness for a year and three months. Although this was by far the loneliest time of my entire life, up till that time I had never felt such closeness to God in all of my life. Not only that, but I wouldn't give away the encounters I had with the Father's heart at this time of my life for anything in the world. God lives in the wilderness because He never leaves us nor forsakes us. As my wife always says, *"Jesus stays with us in the good times and the bad because He's a lover, not a cheater."*

My wound tricked me into believing that my uniqueness forced me into isolation, until I came to the end of my heart wound and decided to embrace truth. I remember the moment distinctly; I was working at a coffee shop at the time serving as a barista. I was standing behind the espresso bar when an old friend of mine from school walked in the coffee shop with her newborn baby. She was with a group of mothers who also had their babies with them. On my break I went to visit my friend who was sitting with the concession of mothers. I sat down with them and held her newborn child. My awareness of the presence of God increased drastically in that moment to the point where I was brought to tears. Looking up, I saw that all eight of the mothers and their babies were covered in golden flakes from head to toe. It was a sign and wonder which pointed me to understanding that God's heart is for family and relationship. Revelation hit me in that moment. After a year and three months of being alone, I understood that I was living life from a place of hurt instead of victory. I realized that it wasn't God's will for me to be a lone ranger, but that I deserved to be part of a family.

Entering the Promised Land of community can be a challenging thing for a lone ranger. It is difficult because a lone ranger desires relationship, yet it's amongst people where their insecurities are triggered. For some of you who are reading this, you have felt misunderstood for who God has created you to be. You have tried to embrace the church, but notice that when you do there is instantly a fear of rejection triggered in your heart. You notice that there is an instant atmosphere of conflict coming from within. When this happens there are two things you can do. You can either withdraw to hide behind your wall of isolation, or you can begin to renew your mind so that you can view these situations from a place of victory.

Unforgiveness engraved within society has trained a lot of us very poorly in how we are to walk in relationships. The world teaches us that when something gets hard, to give up. As soon as conflict stirs, just step away because it's easier to run than to fix. This is why when something comes up in a relationship, we often withdraw and isolate. We become like Pilot when the crowds approached him for a verdict concerning Jesus. Even though responsibility is right in front of us, we just wash our hands of the situation and emotionally disconnect.

It's actually our responsibility to steward the relationships God has given properly, especially when our insecurities begin to surface, therefore creating conflict. Conflict can actually be an incredibly beautiful thing. When my wife and I have a fight or argument, it's more often than not birthed because an insecurity or fear was triggered on one of our parts. Conflict from within actually surfaces the wounding, so that Jesus can heal it. Even though it's uncomfortable, the fruit of conflict is freedom and creation if we learn to deal with it properly.

Embrace the moments that feel stretching and forsake the false shelter of fear that promises fruitless comfort. This is part of learning to overcome a mindset of individualism. In order for us to reach maturity in embracing the family of God, we need to learn to embrace the conflict and sometimes even awkwardness of relationships. We get to be the ones who decide whether the conflict from within will bring good fruit, or separatism. If you find it uncomfortable hanging out in large groups because of a false view on independence, then make an effort to spend time in groups. Embrace the awkwardness and allow Holy Spirit to bring healing. If you feel insecure when you're around fatherly figures, then ask a church leader you know out for coffee. God lives in the awkwardness of a forerunner grafting into the body of Christ.

Honouring Different Personalities And Callings

When God said that a man and woman would marry and become one flesh, He meant this in more than a sexual way. Genesis 1:27 says, *"So God created them in His image; in the image of God He created him; male and female He created them"*. Man alone couldn't bear the complete image of God. So, God created woman to come along side of man that they would represent the fullness of God's image. In marriage, both man and woman progress in becoming one flesh, one person. When a husband and wife come together they need to live in perfect transparency. They can't hide anything of who they are, just as Adam and Eve were completely naked (transparent) and shameless in doing so. Since they were shameless, this tells us that there was no fear that one would face rejection from the other. They lived perfectly open lives receiving one another in the entirety of their beings. The moment we begin to fear rejection we start to hide the parts of ourselves we consider flaws. Instantly walls and masks are put up within the relationship to try and hide what we fear will be rejected. When this happens even in a marriage it is impossible to be one flesh and one person with our spouse. We simply become individuals who live life alongside one another.

Jesus prayed to the Father in John 17:20-21; He said, *"I do not pray for these alone, but also for those who will believe in Me through their word; that they all may be one, as You, Father, are in Me, and I in You; that they also may be one in Us, that the world may believe that You sent Me."* We need to understand the Oneness of the Godhead if we are to understand how to become one flesh in the body of Christ. Just as it is supposed to be in a marriage, the Godhead lives in perfect transparency, never lacking in truth or vulnerability. John 5 shows us that the Father loves the Son and shows Him ALL that He does. Nothing was hidden from the Son. Likewise, Jesus was sinless, so therefore hid nothing from His Father. He allowed His Father to see the very depths of who He was.

Jesus prayed that we the body would be one as He and the Father were one. God's relationship with Himself as a Trinity is the template of what our relationships are supposed to look like within the body of Christ. Jesus was family with the Father before He was God's prophet or teacher. It's time for us to put down the titles and see each other as family before co-labourers. We need to know each other by name before ministerial title. When we are stuck in the past, we fear what the future holds. When we fear the future, we lack in committing to the key relationships that we have in the present. Jesus prayed that no walls would be put up to create any individualism or extreme independence, but instead prayed that the body would become so close that we would exist as one flesh, one person.

In order for the body to walk in this depth of unity, there needs to be an increase of the church honouring God's diversity in the creation of mankind. The reason why there are cliques within churches is because people have a tendency to gravitate to those who are similar to themselves. Jesus shows us through His ministry the importance of different people walking together as one family.

Let's take a look at the 12 disciples for instance: Jesus' disciple Andrew was Peter's brother. He was a fisherman and originally was a disciple of John the Baptist (Mark 1:16-18). James, John and Peter were all fishermen. Many scholars believe that Nathaniel was the only disciple who came from royal blood, or noble birth. They believe this because his name means 'son of Talmai'. Talmai was king of Geshur whose daughter, Maacah, was the wife of David, mother of Absalom (2 Samuel 3:3). Simon was a zealot, which was a conspiracy group that revolted against the government. Many scholars believe that Jude was also part of this group. Matthew was a tax collector, and little is known about the back history of the last five disciples.

This is astounding to me, Jesus picked a man who was from royal blood and threw him with a bunch of fishermen which was one of the lowliest trades in that time. He grabbed a tax collector who worked for the government and put him together with two zealots who in modern times would probably be known as terrorists. Jesus brought together 12 people who didn't only have different personalities, but had completely different ideologies all together. They all perceived life through entirely different lenses, yet Jesus brought them together to teach them how to be a family. Jesus as a Pastor taught them how to live life amongst one another because they were called to be Jesus' successors in leading the revival which redirected history. Sometimes we forget that the same 12 disciples, who walked with Jesus in the gospels, were the same 12 apostles who led the church in Acts, minus Judas. Worldwide revival was actually dependant on whether or not Jesus could teach the 12 to put aside their differences and be a family.

The last supper is one of the most beautiful depictions of unity and fellowship written in the Bible. We see 12 people eating together who from a realistic point of view should not be in relationship with one another. Throughout the gospels we can see how the disciples clearly didn't get along all of the time. In fact, there are several accounts of them arguing amongst each other. Considering their differences how couldn't they? Nathaniel could have been somewhat pretentious, where the fishermen were probably on the rougher side in their personalities. Matthew, being a tax collector could have had problems with superiority and the zealots more than likely had ridiculous authority issues. Yet they could live life together because they met around Jesus. He was their common ground to relate and love one another.

Back in Biblical times, people wouldn't get together to eat with just anyone like we do today. Fellowshipping over food was something special. In that time and culture people would only eat with those who they were committed to living life with. The communion is a picture of 12 men who committed to living life with one another. Jesus brought these men together and taught them to love one another despite their differences to the point where they could commit to each other and be a family. Where at first Jesus had to stand as the mediator between the disciples, by the time He ascended to heaven, they loved each other so much that they could operate as a healthy family to steward revival.

There needs to be a revelation of honour that grips the church if we are going to see a unified move of God. Honour needs to be woven into how we react to people who believe in different doctrines. We need to honour people to the extent that we can differentiate them from the doctrine they believe. If someone believes doctrine that we deem as 'bad', that doesn't make them a bad person. I've heard some leaders of the church say that they won't even sit down beside another leader because they don't agree with their doctrine. This form of stubbornness is probably one of the quickest ways to separatism and disunity within the church. The labels of common day Pharisees and Sadducees are thrown around so flippantly that it's folly. We don't realize that while calling someone a Pharisee, we are actually speaking from a pharicidical mindset. We are acting pharicidical by viewing people through an Old Covenant lens by judging people based on what they do and say instead of honouring them for who they are. They are righteous and separate from imperfection through grace. We need to stop the accusations and need to begin to meet around Jesus instead of stumbling over each other's secondary and tertiary doctrines. When we criticize and distance ourselves from people because of our differences, we are cutting off our ability to receive from God the gift that is them. Many of my close friends in ministry and I disagree on some of our secondary doctrines, but we never allow disrespect to creep into our relationships. We honour one another for

who we are in Christ as we meet around Jesus who is
perfect theology and our primary doctrine.

Babel Restored

Genesis 11:1-8: *"Now the whole earth had one
language and one speech. And it came to pass, as they
journeyed from the east, that they found a plain in the
land of Shinar, and they dwelt there. Then they said to
one another, 'Come let us make bricks and bake them
thoroughly.' They had brick for stone, and they had
asphalt for mortar. And they said, 'Come, let us build
ourselves a city, and a tower whose top is in the
heavens; let us make a name for ourselves, lest we be
scattered abroad over the face of the whole earth.'"*

*"But the Lord came down to see the city and the tower
which the sons of men had built. And the Lord said,
'indeed the people are one and they all have one
language, and this is what they begin to do, now nothing
that they propose to do will be withheld from them.
Come let Us go down and there confuse their language,
that they may not understand one another's speech.' So
the Lord scattered them abroad from there over the face
of all the earth, and they ceased building the city."*

The incident with the fall of Babel was the initial
mass descent of unity for mankind. Those who partook
in building the tower joined in unity to build a tower that

would reach the heavens. Their motivation in building was to create a name for themselves to be a people of renown. God saw that their motives were corrupt since they coveted placement in heaven to have great names; so therefore scattered them and confused their speech by giving new languages.

The cross brought restoration to every curse which was put into fruition under the Old Covenant. Acts 2:1-6 says: *"When the Day of Pentecost had fully come, they were all with one accord in one place. And suddenly there came a sound from heaven, as of a rushing mighty wind, and it filled the whole house where they were sitting. Then there appeared to them divided tongues, as of fire, and one sat upon each of them. And they were all filled with the Holy Spirit and began to speak with other tongues, as the Spirit gave them utterance. And there were dwelling in Jerusalem Jews, devout men, from every nation under heaven. And when this sound occurred, the multitudes came together, and were confused, because everyone heard them speak in his own language."*

Notice how it says that those who came were devout men from every nation under heaven and that everyone heard the believers speak in his own language. See, where at the tower of Babel everyone was scattered and given new tongues, when Holy Spirit poured out at Pentecost, all men of different tongues were assembled and there was clear understanding. In the Old Testament the nations were scattered; in the New Testament the nations are gathered. In this moment, the disunity which took place at Babel was reversed and restored. Even when the Babylonians were unified for corrupt purposes, God said of them, *"Now nothing that they propose to do will be withheld from them."* How much more capable should we be of seeing sustained revival globally as we continue to embrace one another in unity?

Statistics say that in a city of 1,000,000 people there will be approximately 1,666 churches. This is astounding to me considering how 120 people stewarded revival so well that it brought transformation to the nations. Our lack of revelation concerning the family of God has prevented us from already seeing entire cities and nations transformed.

In the book of Revelation there is record of John the Beloved writing apostolic letters to the seven churches (Revelation 2, 3). Look at how John addresses each church. John didn't write a separate letter for every small congregation in Ephesus. He didn't write a separate letter to every house church in Sardis. One apostle could write one letter to the church of Ephesus and the entire church within that region would be notified. John didn't have to write a separate letter to 'First Sardis Assembly' because they were in conflict with the 'Full Sardis Church'. There was such a revelation of kingdom relationships where entire regions were unified around Christ.

Acts 2:46: *"So continuing daily with one accord in the temple, and breaking bread from house to house, they ate their food with gladness and simplicity of heart."*

The early church would meet and eat together consistently as an act of devoting to live life alongside one another. God is calling His church to commit to unity. It starts with our immediate relationships and will result in regional and global unity amongst the church. Being reconciled to the family of God is a constant process for all of us because there is a persistent temptation to isolate aspects of our individuality from others. Although we may believe there is safety in being alone, God is trying to show us that there is true safety and freedom in unity. You are not alone. You have a family who loves you. Since we were all created unique, there is an aspect of us that differentiates us from our fellow man. Since we all stand alone in our rarity, we may as well learn to receive one another and be the family of God.

Conclusive Wisdom

Marrying The Corners

Matthew 7:24-27: *"Therefore whoever hears these sayings of Mine, and does them, I will liken him to a wise man who built his house on the rock: and the rain descended, the floods came, and the winds blew and beat on that house; and it did not fall, for it was founded on the rock. But everyone who hears these sayings of Mine, and does not do them, will be like a foolish man who built his house on the sand: and the rain descended, the floods came, and the winds blew and beat on that house; and it fell. And great was its fall."*

Since we are currently in a state where God is reintroducing the true foundation of Christ to the global church; apostolic boundaries need to be embraced by the church for the purpose of bringing order. Jesus draws parallel between the wise man who built his house upon the rock and the foolish man who built his house upon the sand. Sand is actually small particles of rock.

What we have tried to often do as the church, is we have tried to take one of these four corners (grace, the kingdom, the Father and the family of God), divorce it from the other three, and then build our belief system upon it. We can't try to build our faith upon truths we have tried to separate from the true foundation. We need to build from a complete perspective of what Jesus taught. This is the only way we can become expert builders. It was Paul's full picture and depth of revelation of who Jesus was that enabled him to build masterfully as an apostle. This is why some ministries reflect only one or two of the four corners through their expression of revival. We have a tendency to gravitate to the truths which provide comfort to our personalities. However, in order to move in excellence to represent the full gospel, we need to see Jesus from different angles.

Let's compare the painter to the sculptor: A painter will take an idea from his mind and will try to duplicate a three-dimensional object onto a two-dimensional canvas. Now, whichever angle you look at the canvas from, the picture will remain the same because it was painted upon something flat. It will forever remain as one piece of art. The sculptor in my opinion takes things to a greater level of excellence. The sculptor takes a three-dimensional idea and sculpts a block of marble into a three-dimensional statue. Whichever angle or perspective you look at the statue it changes. Instead of it remaining the same piece of artwork, it becomes thousands of pieces of art depending on which angle you look at it. A master builder isn't limited by only allowing himself to see

Christ from one or two perspectives. His hunger for truth pushes him to know Christ in wholeness.

Often when a fresh revelation is restored to the church, there are some who will take the pendulum to an extreme. This is the by-product of building upon only one or two corners of the foundation. Every corner actually functions to balance out the other revelatory truths, therefore making it impossible for a revelation to be brought to unhealthy extremes. We should never embrace revelation which disagrees with foundational truths. Jesus is the foundation. He is the strong rock. Any revelation that we receive should never contradict the foundation, otherwise it isn't inspired by Holy Spirit.

When we try to build upon a singular truth instead of the fullness of the foundation, even a legit revelation in its extremity can become destructive. This is why it's important to marry the foundational revelations to one another in our hearts instead of trying to divorce them. It's impossible to swing a revelatory pendulum to an extreme if it's tied to the other three corners because they keep one another centered.

This means that a revelation of grace separate from any of the other three truths can actually be destructive. If we only have an understanding of grace, then we will have a tendency to slip into a mindset which tells us that any form of work is legalism. This will of course lead to patterns of laziness and apathy. We need to marry the grace revelation to the revelation of the kingdom of heaven which teaches that we need to co-labour with God to see heaven invade earth. By doing this, we disarm the pitfalls of extremity. We aren't labouring for righteousness, which comes through grace. Instead we are labouring to see revival. See how they balance one another out? When we carry both revelations, it's actually impossible for us to embrace a grace theology which dismisses personal responsibility. It becomes impossible for us to fall into extreme teachings of grace because the false will clearly contradict other truths pertaining to the gospel.

In the same way, if we carry a revelation of the kingdom apart from grace, then it is likely that we will begin to live from an Old Covenant perspective. We will walk in an Old Covenant mindset by labouring for the Father's approval, which dismisses grace, instead of labouring for revival. We need to push for revival from a place of rest, and this can only happen when an understanding of grace and the kingdom can co-labour together.

If we walk in a revelation of the Father's love, then it needs to be balanced out by a revelation of the family of God. If we don't allow both pillars to be built within us, then we could have a profound understanding of intimacy with the Father, but could slip into patterns of isolation. Isolation is an extreme which many Christians have believed to be a form of Christlikeness. Jesus did exemplify times of isolation to be with His Father, but He never modeled a lifestyle of it because it stands in contrast to the truth of the family of God. Most who know how to receive from the Father, but not from the body will have a tendency to slip into doctrines which contradict the cross since they lack accountability. Accountability is the by-product of community. Healthy revelation will never be properly stewarded apart from it. We can start small sparks of revival as individuals, but it's only in unity where we can actually become part of a movement which will impact the masses.

Likewise, if we only regard relationships and not intimacy with the Father, we fail to have true personal breakthrough as a direct result of knowing Him. If we fail to marry the corner of family to the others, all of our revelation will come second hand from others instead of being able to receive straight from the Father's heart. This of course breeds an unhealthy co-dependence. An understanding of family separate from the kingdom will result in a lack of ability to dream bigger than the intricate.

When bound together, the foundation becomes without crack, permitting an unfaltering spiritual house to be built upon it. We become a people who understand that our righteousness through grace leads us to intimacy with the Father. Our relationship with Him reveals our identities, permitting us to partner in unity. This empowers us to see the nations transformed through kingdom expansion.

Holy Spirit wants to shake whichever parts of our theologies that don't reflect the person of Jesus. When all has been shaken which can be shaken, all that's left is the rock on which we can build our house. As leaders whether in the church, our families, business, government, the arts, media or education we would be wise to build upon the whole person of Christ instead of part.

Out Of Tradition And Into Adventure

Genesis 19:24-26: *"Then the LORD rained brimstone and fire on Sodom and Gomorrah, from the LORD out of the heavens. So He overthrew those cities, all the plain, all the inhabitants of the cities, and what grew on the ground. But his wife looked back behind him, and she became a pillar of salt."*

God sought to destroy Sodom and Gomorrah because of their corrupt ways. Lot, finding favour with God was given warning to leave the city before God's wrath was poured out. Lot and his family were given instruction to not look back at Sodom and Gomorrah. However, failing to heed God's word, Lot's wife looked back at the fallen city. As she looked she was turned into a pillar of salt.

The fact that Lot's wife turned into a pillar of salt draws an incredible prophetic teaching for us. The primary purpose of salt isn't to make our food taste good, but actually to preserve food. By looking back at the fallen city, she was trying to preserve her past season when God was calling her to discover new land. This is where many of us wrestle when we are confronted with a new truth or side of Jesus. We are called to discover new land, but we are comfortable in the tradition of our past season of understanding.

I am ending on this point because the truths of Christ which I taught throughout the course of this book may have stretched your revelatory standpoint. However, we need to understand that God is calling forth a generation who will pursue the truths which threaten our normal.

Many of us in our understanding have dwelled in a season which has grown old and familiar. We have resided in a land in which we have become experts. We know the placement of every rock. We know the name of every tree. We have grown comfortable. Yet, there is a flicker of fire within which can only be described as restlessness. We have grown restless because we know that we were created for adventure. It burns within us because we know there is new land to be discovered beyond what our eyes can see. We are being called out of the spiritual nostalgia we carry towards our past seasons of understanding. We can either continue to reside in our past seasons of monotony, out of a fear of the unknown, or take the hand of the most amazing Man who has ever walked the earth into purpose and excitement. Instead of trying to preserve our past realms of comfort, it's time to step out of normality, into adventuring throughout God's eternal nature. There are greater sights for your eyes to behold.

God has called you to discover new lands. He has designed you to build new cities.

Made in the USA
Charleston, SC
20 April 2015